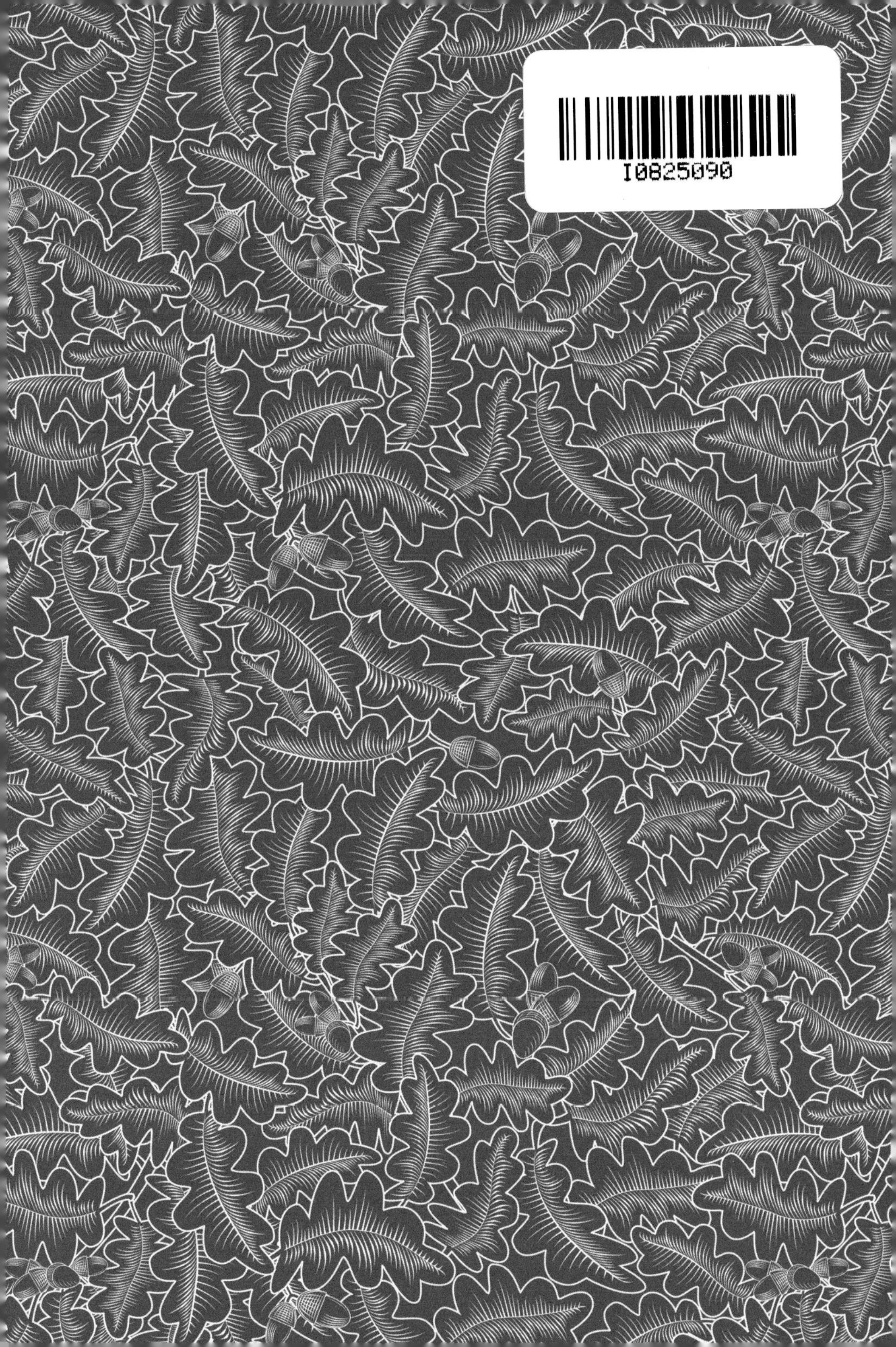
I0825090

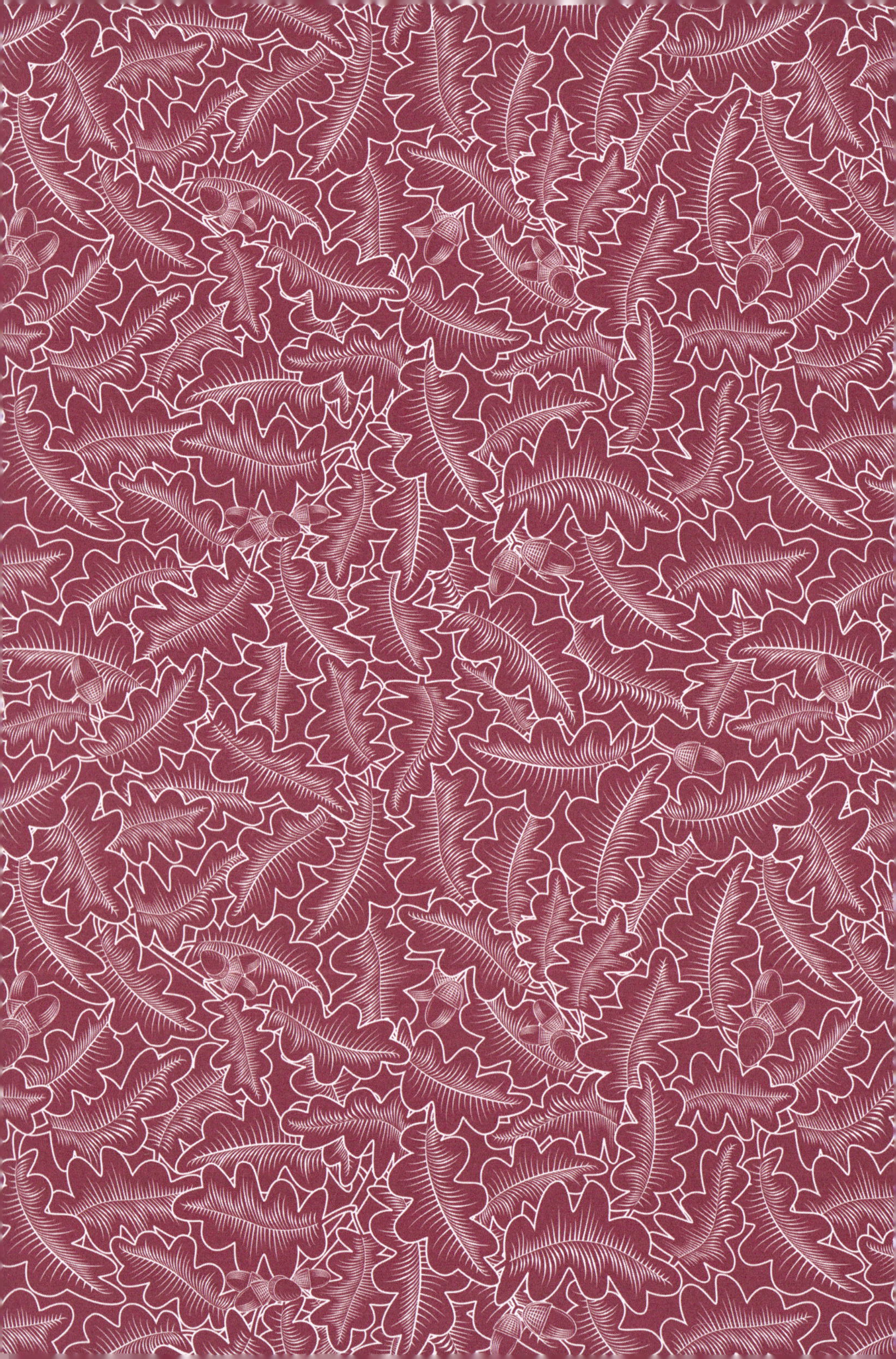

WHITTLING

Wildlife

WHITTLING Wildlife

Peter Benson

Contents

I dedicate this book to all the woodcarving friends that I have worked with around the world and from whom I have learnt so much. Thank you.

Introduction

IN MY PREVIOUS BOOK, *WHITTLING WOODLAND ANIMALS*, I LOOKED AT THE VARIOUS ANIMALS AND BIRDS THAT MIGHT BE FOUND IN WOODLANDS OR THE COUNTRYSIDE. I WANTED IT TO BE POSSIBLE TO MAKE ALL THE PROJECTS USING WOOD THAT COULD EASILY BE OBTAINED, SO THEY WERE DESIGNED TO FIT INTO BASSWOOD OR LIME BLOCKS THAT WERE 1⅛IN (30MM), 1⅝IN (40MM) OR 2IN (50MM) SQUARE AND 6IN (150MM) LONG. THESE SIZES ARE READILY AVAILABLE ON THE INTERNET.

Left to right: polar bear cub, beaver and walrus.

This book is a companion volume to *Whittling Woodland Animals*. I have worked with the same design parameters but the subjects have been chosen from animals, birds and other creatures that might be found in or near water. The scope is enormous but, when I was faced with the same limitations on the size of the wood to be used, and with subjects that would be practical to carve using mostly a knife, my choice was drastically reduced.

I have tried to offer projects that are suitable for beginners, right through to experienced carvers, and they are arranged in what I feel is the order of difficulty. Having said that, there is nothing to stop you from scaling up any of the carvings or making them more complicated. Consider my offerings as a starting point and feel free to make of them what you wish.

In a book of this size there is also a limit to the number of projects that can be included. Here you will find 15 to choose from, with the basic steps to enable you to finish each piece. The projects do not contain a complete list of cut-for-cut instructions as that would involve much more than could fit into a book of this type, so you will need some detailed reference material to check the

anatomy and symmetry in order to get a realistic result. There are myriad photos of the subjects available in books or on the internet for reference, and you could take your own photos of those animals that you are able to see for yourself.

Just one small point here. Copyright laws don't allow you to copy anyone else's work or pictures for your own financial benefit. You will probably get away with it if you never sell or exhibit your work, but I question the ethics of this. Obviously, a book like this invites readers to copy the designs and develop them in their own way but using them commercially is not allowed.

The main thing is to have fun and carve safely. Remember, what you are working with is only a piece of wood, worth very little. If it doesn't come up to expectations, you have only spent your time and, hopefully, enjoyed the process. Start again and use what you have learnt to make the next piece better!

A small set of gouges and a folding knife can fit into a spectacle case.

Tools and equipment

THE FIRST FEW PROJECTS CAN BE COMPLETED WITH LITTLE MORE THAN A SHARP KNIFE AND A SAFETY GLOVE BUT, AS YOU PROGRESS, YOU WILL NEED A FEW MORE TOOLS TO GET THE RESULTS YOU WANT. YOU CAN MANAGE WITH A SMALL SELECTION THAT CAN BE CONTAINED IN A NORMAL SPECTACLE CASE, MAKING THEM VERY EASY TO CARRY AROUND. IN FACT, THE TOOLS AND WOOD FOR EACH PROJECT CAN EASILY FIT INTO A NORMAL POCKET.

CUTTING TOOLS

Most projects in this book will benefit from having the pattern cut from the wood with a band saw, but this can also be done with a coping saw or similar.

GOUGES

Once the pattern has been cut out, a small selection of palm gouges will be needed to get into the more difficult-to-reach places. Although I am generally reluctant to recommend tools to readers, I have found the range of palm gouges from Ashley Iles and Pfeil to be excellent, along with the very slim-handled detail tools available from Dockyard and Ashley Iles. Carving while holding the wood in your hand can be rather dangerous with the

A coping saw can be used to cut out the patterns.

A set of palm gouges is needed for getting into hard-to-reach places.

wrong tools, and these all have short blades with either little chunky handles, or thin pencil-type handles, which can be held in a pen or pencil grip, proving very safe to use.

I would advise against purchasing some of the very cheap imported sets of tools that are widely advertised, as I have found them very difficult to get sharp enough to cut anything and, even when I have managed to get an edge on one, the tool very soon becomes blunt. I must admit, though, that I was given a set of ten Japanese tools that was less than half the cost of one normal tool, and, when I eventually decided to try them, I was amazed at how good they were, even though the range of gouge shapes was not that extensive. Unfortunately, when you buy sets of tools you will get quite a few that you will never use.

The answer, I suppose, is to try what you can and make your own decisions. There are many different tools available on the internet for very little money, and, if you haven't had the opportunity to try any of them beforehand, it might be worth taking a chance. You won't lose a great deal of money and you may even be able to send them back. Cost is not always a good guide to value – there are tools for sale out there at considerable cost that I wouldn't feel able to recommend to anyone. Do your homework and work with what you can afford and feel most comfortable using. There is just one point here: all the most well-known companies that make carving tools will guarantee them for life. If you become serious about the activity, that can be quite an advantage.

KNIVES

Many of you will have already been whittling for some time and will own suitable knives but, if you are new to this craft, I have a few tips for you if you are planning to buy knives for the first time.

First of all, don't buy a set of knives that all have the same type of handle. Whittling can be quite hard on the hands if done for a long period of time. Holding a handle over a prolonged period can cause hand cramps that can be very painful. This can be avoided if you frequently change to a knife with a different-shaped handle as it will change the position of the fingers, reducing the likelihood of cramps. My advice is to get a basic knife, and another of a different shape, work with them and see how it goes. If possible, try as many different styles as you can – you don't have to spend a lot of money – and you will find, as you go along, that you prefer a particular blade shape and range of handles. You can then buy a more expensive one, if you wish.

The really important thing about any knife you use is to keep it as sharp as you possibly can – see pages 16–17 to learn how to do this.

Use knives with different-shaped handles to prevent hand cramps.

This Beavercraft knife is good value; note the rounded-off end.

Whatever knife you use, you need to be aware of any legal implications of knife ownership. If you only intend to carve at home, you can use any knife that you wish. However, if you intend to carry the knife on your person in public in the UK, you can only carry a folding (not locking) knife with a blade less than 3in (75mm) long. Fixed-blade knives of all types are not permissible. If you are living outside the UK, you will need to check the laws in the country you reside in.

I started with a simple folding penknife and still use it from time to time. It might be worth looking in boot fairs or flea markets for second-hand penknives as they will nearly all be quite suitable. You can usually find something online as well that is not too expensive. As long as they are comfortable to hold and are capable of being sharpened to a fine edge, they will last you for years and save you a lot of money.

When you have been carving for a while, you will have a clear idea of what is best for you and you can then spend your money wisely. I have recently been teaching a group of children to carve and have found a small, cheap knife from Beavercraft that has proved to be very good value and keeps its edge for long periods. I am sure that there are others that are similar if you are prepared to browse (see page 141 for a list of recommended suppliers).

One important safety aspect to note here is that most knives come with a very sharp point. The Beavercraft knife is no exception and I have rounded off the end for my classes with the children. This doesn't affect the cutting efficiency but it does avoid any possibility of a stabbing cut.

To summarize the tool situation, what you use is very much a matter of what you feel happy with and that will do what you want. If you intend to travel around, you might like to make up a simple set that will fit into your pocket. I have a folding knife that will fit into a simple spectacle case yet will do all that I need.

SAFETY EQUIPMENT

While the correct tool can minimize the risk of injury, accidents can easily happen and I think it is madness to do this kind of carving without wearing a suitable safety glove on one or both hands. I have been teaching a small group of children (9–11 year olds) to carve for nearly a year now without any injury and they wouldn't consider picking up a knife without their gloves on. (I hope this isn't tempting fate!)

Safety gloves should be worn at all times.

There are many suppliers of suitable gloves but please make sure that you have ones that are cut level 5 at least – it should state what they are on the glove. The standard for these varies from Europe to the USA but check that whatever you are using does the job. Beware of cheap gloves with spurious claims as I have cut some of these in half with a knife very easily just to check how good they are. Get good ones, preferably from a company that specializes in safety equipment, and they will last you for ages.

A leather apron is also recommended to prevent injury.

I also recommend that you wear a leather apron while carving as it is possible to do a lot of damage by cutting your legs if you are holding your carving in your lap. A supply of plasters (band aids) is also advisable as even the smallest of nicks to the fingers can be rather messy.

ABRASIVES

You can use any abrasive that you have to hand but the wood you are using is fairly soft, so don't use coarse abrasives or you will end up with deep scratches all over your work. Keep the grades to 150 grit or finer, and move on to a finer grit until you have the result you want.

Sanding will double the carving time and I would only do it if you are prepared to make the effort, although do bear in mind that a finish (see opposite) will show up any marks left on the surface.

FINISHING

Once you have completed your carving, it will need some sort of finish. The choice of finish is largely up to you and what kind of look you want your completed work to have. You can give the whole thing a coat or two of finishing oil, which will dry to a good protective surface. If you like the finish you get from varnish, that is another option, or you can simply apply a coat of wax polish.

If you prefer to colour the finished carving, I think the best results are obtained with acrylic watercolour paint, diluted to get the shade you want, or by using Procion fabric dyes. These can give you some very bright, attractive colours without hiding the texture of the wood – to get the same effect with paint will hide any wood grain completely. There are several other methods of tinting the wood, some of which are described in the projects, but I would advise against using wood stain as this is very difficult to control on small carvings. I ruined a few of my carvings in the early days, when I didn't know of any alternatives.

Suitable wood

YOU CAN, OF COURSE, CARVE IN ANY WOOD YOU LIKE. I RECKON, OVER MY LIFETIME OF CARVING, THAT I HAVE TRIED MOST OF THEM. SOME ARE GOOD, SOME NOT BAD AND SOME ARE ABSOLUTELY AWFUL! YOUR CHOICE WILL BE GOVERNED BY HOW STRONG YOUR HANDS ARE AND HOW LONG YOU WANT TO SPEND ON A PIECE. THE HARDER AND MORE CLOSE-GRAINED THE WOOD IS, THE BETTER THE FINISH WILL BE, BUT THE SMALLER THE CHIPS THAT YOU CAN REMOVE.

I have chosen basswood for most of these projects as it is relatively easy to get hold of in small quantities and is also not too difficult to carve, yet will give a reasonable finish and take most of the detail that you will want to include. Basswood (*Tilia americana*) is a member of the lime family and can be difficult to distinguish from English lime *(Tilia vulgaris*), which is traditionally considered to be the carver's wood. For some reason, it is difficult to find many suppliers advertising lime for sale but the wood I have bought as basswood is fine for carving these projects and could well be lime – it doesn't matter either way.

If you are not worried about any grain pattern, you could try jelutong (*Dyera costulata*, the tree from which latex is obtained for making rubber). This can be quite a bit softer than lime, but, like all woods, will get considerably harder as it gets older.

When choosing a wood to use, you have to accept that, if you want something to be easy to carve, you do have to make some sacrifices. The softer the wood, the more difficult it is to keep the work neat while you are carving, and you shouldn't try to add too much fine detail unless you are prepared to spend a considerable amount of time cleaning up. For small carvings I prefer to use a much harder wood that will accept very fine detail, but the time taken to finish such a piece can be up to ten times longer than with a softer wood. If you want to try a harder wood you could use boxwood (*Buxus sempervirens*), lemonwood (*Pittosporum eugenioides*) or any of the fruitwoods such as apple (*Malus sylvestris*), pear (*Pyrus communis*), plum (*Prunus domestica*) or cherry (*Prunus avium*). These are delightful to carve and, I think, worth the extra effort but they are not really suitable for most beginners.

The block sizes I used for my carvings are shown in each project but you can make yours from whatever size you wish. Sources of basswood proliferate on the internet but most pre-cut blocks are too small. I got my supply from Andrew Legge (see page 141) and he will cut to size for anyone ordering in the UK. For those of you living abroad, I'm sure you can find a suitable supplier if you do a little research. If you are based in the USA, look for northern basswood from Minnesota or Wisconsin for the best results.

A WORD OF WARNING

If you are whittling with a knife, I certainly wouldn't recommend that you use any old piece of wood you have found in the shed or the local countryside. Dead wood can be very hard and there are some horrible woods out there that may be ideal for furniture but are a nightmare to carve. Also, many exotic or diseased woods can be highly toxic, particularly if sanded, so they should be avoided. For what it costs, get something decent – you will be happy that you did!

ADVICE FOR BEGINNERS

If you are new to knife carving, don't carve for too long at a time to begin with, and don't try to take off too much with each cut. Relax and enjoy the process and don't worry about how long it takes. If you want results in a hurry, you are better off working in clay or with watercolours. Build up gradually until your hands and fingers become accustomed to the process and remember that the sharper your knife, the easier it is (see pages 16–17 for advice on sharpening).

Sharpening

BEFORE YOU START TRYING TO CUT INTO YOUR PRECIOUS PIECE OF WOOD, YOU NEED TO MAKE SURE THAT YOUR TOOLS ARE SUITABLE FOR THE JOB AND THAT YOU WON'T BE WASTING TIME TRYING TO GET A DECENT FINISH. THERE ARE MANY WOULD-BE CARVERS OUT THERE WHO STRUGGLE, AND PROBABLY GIVE UP, BECAUSE THEY HAVE SUCH A HARD JOB GETTING ANYWHERE. THEY THINK IT IS THEIR LACK OF ABILITY WHEN ALL THAT IS WRONG IS THAT THEIR TOOLS ARE BLUNT.

How, then, do you know if the tool is sharp? First of all, when buying a tool ask if it is sharpened as some will only have ground edges. Look at the bevel – if it shows grinding marks, it will not be sharp. A sharpened and honed blade will have a very smooth and shiny bevel.

Test the blade by running it along a piece of wood; if you get a clean shaving the blade is sharp.

One good test is to get a small piece of the wood that you intend to carve, choose an edge of the piece at one end and, holding the knife or gouge lightly in your fingertips, run the tool along the edge and see if you can produce a clean shaving. If you can, the tool is sharp; if not, it needs to be sharpened. Do not test it by cutting paper or the hairs on your arm, as some suggest, as even a relatively blunt tool will do that.

HOW TO SHARPEN

Assuming that some sharpening is necessary, what should you do? First you need to look at the bevel on each face of the blade – it may be flat or slightly convex (curved upwards). For both of these it is important that the surface immediately behind the cutting edge

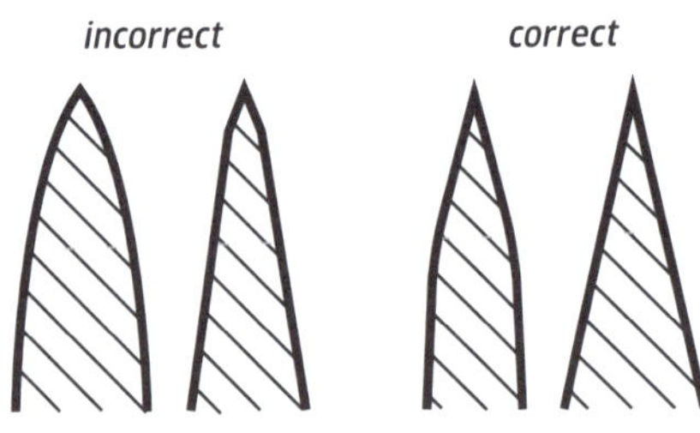

Knife blades.

The bevel can be flattened on a leather strop.

Gouges can be sharpened on MDF boards.

should be flat for at least ⅛in (3mm) –see diagram (below left). If this is not the case, it will need to be corrected with some form of abrasive. The options are an oilstone, a diamond plate, an abrasive sheet of wet and dry paper or emery cloth, or perhaps even a belt sander or similar. If you don't own any of these, you may be able to get an engineer or woodworker to do this for you.

Once this is achieved, it is important to maintain this throughout the time it is used. This can be done quite easily by stropping (or honing), particularly with the knife, on a leather strop. The strop should be dressed with an abrasive compound (chrome cleaner is ideal) and the blade run along the surface, with the edge trailing and the bevel flat to the leather. Do this for around six or eight passes to get rid of any roughness at the edge and the knife should be ready. This will need to be done after about every half an hour of use to get the best from the tool.

While the same process can be used to sharpen gouges, I have found that by far the best way to keep them up to scratch is to use a small piece of MDF (medium density fibreboard). Cut a groove in the surface of the board with the tool you intend to sharpen, and then drag the tool backwards through the groove a few times, keeping the angle constant. No abrasive is needed but you will need a to make a new groove for each different tool. This is particularly good for V-tools as it will hone the whole of the cutting surface. Again, you will need to do this frequently for best results.

Like most skills, you will get better at sharpening as you go along and it will soon become second nature for you to keep your tools in the right condition.

Using the knife

THERE ARE INHERENT DANGERS IN WHITTLING WITH A KNIFE THAT DON'T GENERALLY OCCUR IN MORE TRADITIONAL METHODS OF CARVING WITH GOUGES, CHISELS AND MALLETS WHERE THE WORK IS HELD IN A VICE OR CLAMP. WHEN WHITTLING, THE WOOD IS HELD IN ONE HAND WHILE IT IS CUT WITH A KNIFE HELD IN THE OTHER. CONSEQUENTLY, THERE ARE MANY OPPORTUNITIES FOR THE KNIFE TO SLIP FROM THE WOOD AND CAUSE INJURY IF THE CORRECT PROCEDURES ARE NOT FOLLOWED.

HOLDING THE KNIFE

There are several ways to hold a knife, which are used in different situations.

The forward grip

This is the same grip you would use when sharpening a pencil and can be used for simple paring, removing very thin slivers of wood. It can also be used when cutting into a stop cut. You can use this with the thumb round the handle or along the back of the blade.

The backward grip

This grip is done with the cutting edge facing the body and should be used with care. It is useful for small cuts made with a pulling action and it is advised to use thumb protection.

The middle or downward grip

This grip is halfway between the first two and is generally used to cut directly into the surface of the wood like cutting a slice of bread or chopping vegetables.

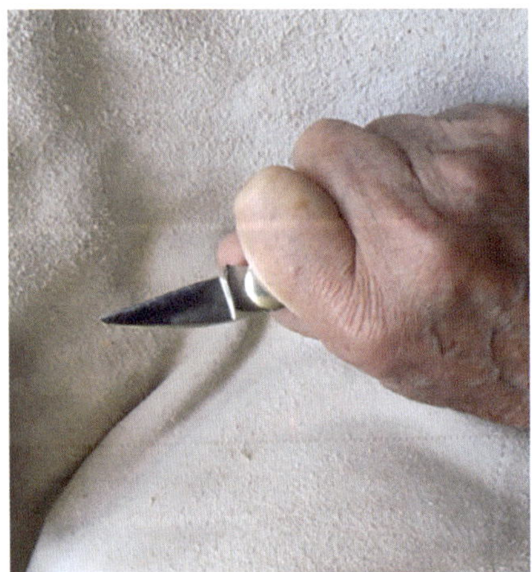

The forward grip.

The forward grip while making a stop cut.

SAFETY PRECAUTIONS

There are many obvious precautions that can be taken to minimize the possibility of accidents and allow the carver to enjoy the process.

1 Keeping the knife sharp by regular honing on a leather strop will minimize the likelihood of slipping.

2 Always put down the knife when not in use. Scratching your nose with a knife in your hand can be disastrous!

3 Similarly, talking to someone with a knife in your hand is not advised.

4 If a knife or tool rolls off the bench or table, don't try to catch it or stop it with your foot. I have seen some very nasty gashes in hands or legs when people do this.

5 There are some good ways that you can use your knife and some that are not so good. Check the following notes on the best ways to hold the knife and the basic cuts to use. If you get into good practices then you will have a happy and safe life of whittling.

The backward grip.

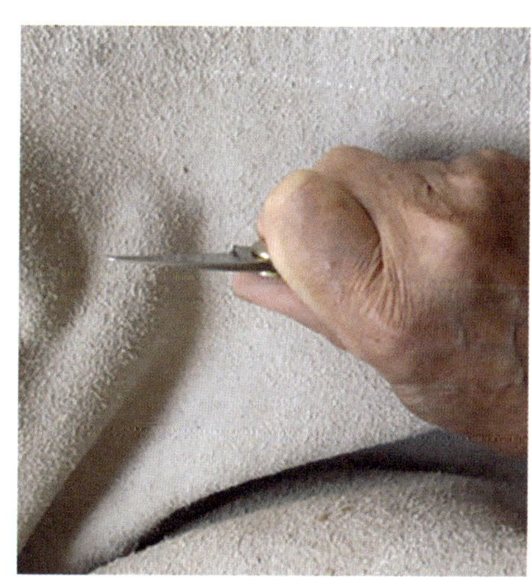

The middle or downward grip.

Making a wedge cut.

Using a wedge as a stop cut.

THE BASIC CUTS

There are three basic cuts that you will need to know for whittling.

The wedge cut

This is used to cut into the surface of the wood with two cuts at an angle like a V. This forms what is known as a **stop cut**. You can safely cut either way into the V, with no danger of the blade slipping out of the wood. This cut can be used to remove large quantities of waste wood.

The paring cut

This can be used with a forward or backward grip and is used to cut along the grain, generally away from the body, removing a thin sliver of wood. Used in conjunction with a stop cut (see above), you can also remove a large amount of waste wood by allowing the wood to split as you cut, thus saving a lot of energy.

Extra pressure can be applied by putting the thumb of your supporting hand on the back of the blade and pushing, or using it as a fulcrum and pulling back with the knife hand and cutting with a lever action.

The pull cut

This is really a squeezing action and involves cutting towards the thumb. It should only be used to remove small amounts of wood and usually only when there are problems with access or grain direction. Wear a thumb guard (readily available online) to protect your thumb from cuts while whittling.

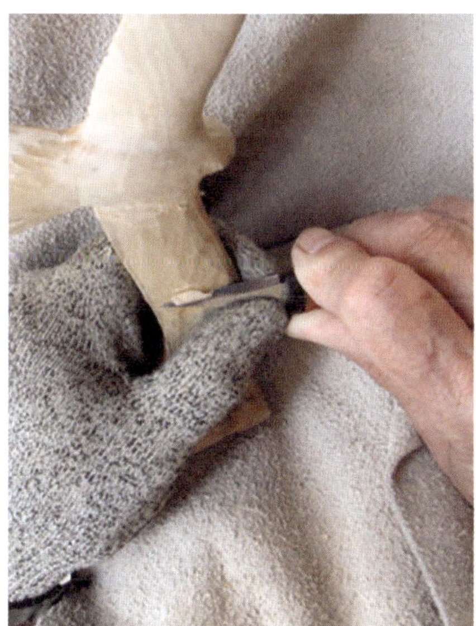

The paring cut.

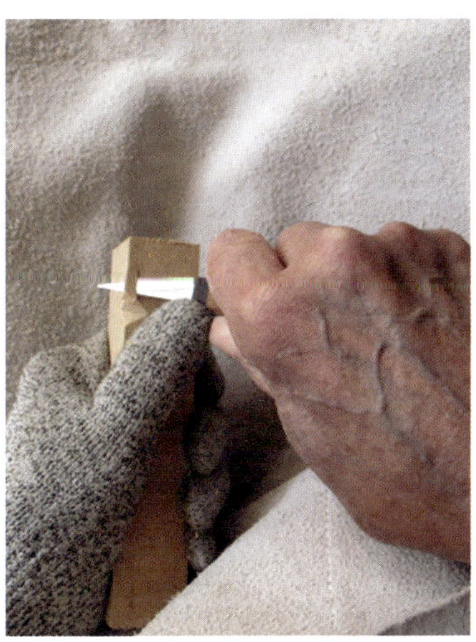

Apply extra pressure to a paring cut using the thumb of your supporting hand.

These are my suggestions for using the knife but you will no doubt work out ways that best suit you. The main thing is to work safely as there is nothing more likely to put you off whittling than a badly cut hand! And remember that a sharp knife cuts more easily than a dull one, so you will need to hone it regularly – after about every half hour of carving time.

TIP

While the knife is in contact with the wood it is generally safe. When in the air it is wild and dangerous. I recommend that you keep your arms in contact with the body or table and move the knife as little as possible. Try moving the wood instead of moving the knife. After a little practice, you will find this a much easier way of removing wood.

The pull cut.

Dealing with the eyes

ALMOST EVERY CARVER I HAVE COME ACROSS HAS HAD A PROBLEM WITH KNOWING HOW TO MAKE THE EYES ON A CARVING LOOK REASONABLY LIFELIKE. AS A RESULT, ADDING THE EYES IS VERY OFTEN LEFT UNTIL THE CARVING IS ALMOST COMPLETE BUT THIS MEANS THE STRESS INVOLVED IS INCREASED CONSIDERABLY. AS ALL THE SUBJECTS IN THIS BOOK HAVE EYES, I FELT I NEEDED TO SHOW THE OPTIONS THAT ARE AVAILABLE TO YOU.

POINTS TO CONSIDER

To begin with, there are a few points about eyes that may be obvious but need to be understood.

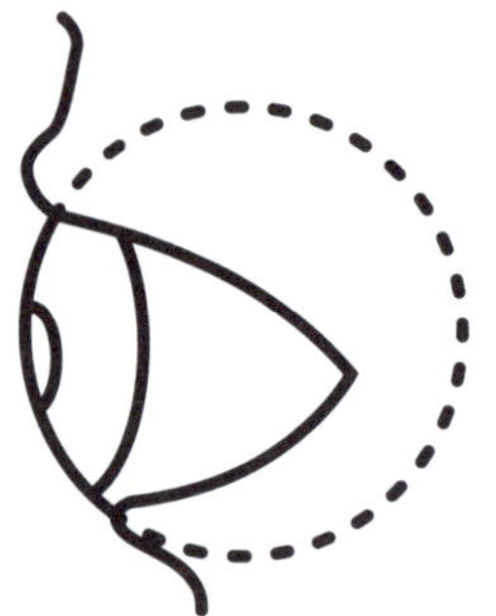

Diagram of the eye.

Round glass eyes are a good option for carvings of fish.

The eye is pretty well a complete sphere and how it is set in the head varies according to the creature involved. Hunters' eyes will generally face forwards as they need to be able to focus on prey. Only half of the eye, between the eyelids, will be visible from the side. Prey animals' eyes are usually placed more to the sides of the head so that they can see all around them, particularly to the rear. All of the open parts of the eye will be visible from the side.

The visible parts of most mammal and bird eyes are not round and have clearly defined eyelids, the top one further forward and covering more of the eye than the bottom one (see diagram). This means that the bottom of the eye appears to be further back than the top.

Fish, reptiles and amphibians tend to have round eyes with no clearly visible eyelids. These lend themselves to the addition of glass eyes, which are easy to fit.

Whichever eyes you intend to add, the front surface of the area should be vertical and domed, showing that it is part of the sphere before you think about carving the actual shape of the open eye.

Once you have the domed shape, you need to draw the outline of each eye, making sure that they are an exact match for shape and position in the head. If they are circular, you can use a suitably sized gouge to cut the outline – all gouges with a sweep from 3 to 9 will cut an accurate circle if carefully turned, end on, in the surface of the wood – you just need one of the right size and sweep. For eyes that are not circular, you can draw the shape, cut along the lines using a knife or V-tool and then round off the area inside these lines. This should give a good effect.

Larger eyes can be carved and then painted.

DIFFERENT METHODS OF ADDING EYES

As most of the projects in this book involve small animals, you might well decide to 'suggest' the eyes rather than try to carve them. After all, you probably wouldn't see much more than a line or shadow where the eyes would be; see the beaver (pages 110–115) and cormorant (pages 48–53) as examples.

You can, of course, simply use a small drop of black paint to represent the eye. For a larger eye you can carve it and then paint it, either with gloss paint or with matt acrylic and then add a drop of clear nail varnish to give it a high gloss – I have used this technique many times and have generally been very happy with the result.

Eyes can be made from small dowels of material in a contrasting colour.

I find that it is easier to use a knife or scalpel to scrape the horn rather than cutting it.

A very realistic eye can be obtained by drilling a small hole and inserting a small dowel made from a contrasting wood, a piece of dark plastic or buffalo horn (which is easy to carve to the shape you need). Buffalo horn in particular polishes up well but does take a little care and patience. I have dropped several eyes onto the floor and spent some time on my hands and knees over the years, but the result is worthwhile.

I find it less stressful to partially cut the dowel to the required size and then glue it in place in the drilled hole. When the glue has set, you can complete the cut, leaving a slightly ragged surface to the eye. With careful sanding and polishing, a very effective eye will be the result, and this method can be used for even the tiniest of eyes.

If, however, you want to add a very small brown or amber eye, you are in the realms of the miniature carvers. Using the same method, you can, first of all, insert a small piece of coloured plastic or amber dowel of the right size and then drill an even smaller hole for the black pupil, which can be made from black wood or horn. If you are using amber, you can even just paint the black pupil on the back of the eye as it will show through. You will probably need quite a bit of practice to get this right, but it is worth it.

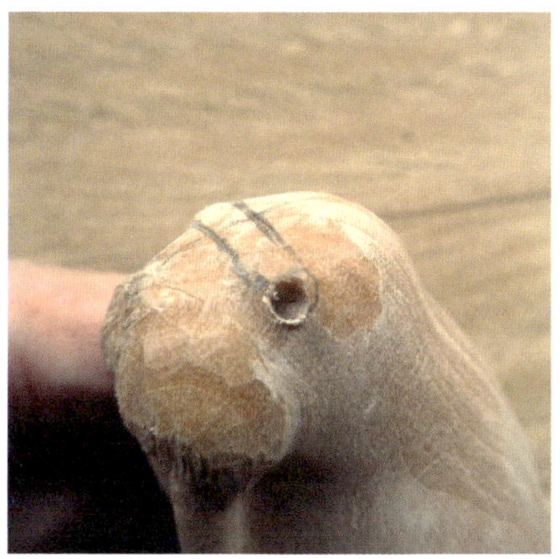

After the hole is drilled, the longer dowel is placed inside and then trimmed, sanded and polished. The part to be inserted can be partly separated beforehand to simplify the process.

Small eyes can be made from wooden, plastic, horn or amber dowels in a contrasting colour.

MATCHING EYES

One of the main problems that carvers have when trying to add a realistic or even plain carved eye is in trying to match one eye to the other. Usually, this involves either numerous attempts at drawing them both to look the same, or carving one eye and then trying to get the other to match endless unsuccessful times, gradually getting further and further back in the head until giving up in despair!

A solution I have found is to get a sticky label, colour it and fold it in half before cutting out the shape you want. When unfolded, you will have a pair of matching shapes representing a left and right eye. By sticking these on your carving, you can adjust them as much as you like until they look right, without making a single cut. Once you're happy, you can draw around your shapes and carve the outlines of the eyes stress free.

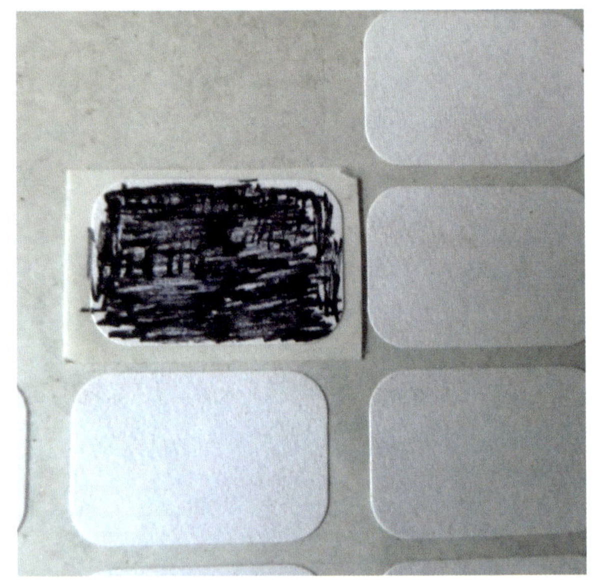

A sticky label folded in half can help you achieve matching eyes.

This method helped me fix a problem with the octopus carving.

I did this with the octopus and found an added bonus: when I stuck the patterns on, I noticed that one dome I had carved for the eyes was different from the other. I removed the patterns, reshaped the dome and tried again.

Having said all this, if you are carving small subjects, it may not be practical to carve eyes at all and, if you try, you may spoil an otherwise beautiful carving. Unless you really want the subject to look particularly realistic, it may be better to 'suggest' the eyes or paint them.

Practical advice

UNLESS YOU READ THROUGH OR CARVE ALL THE PROJECTS IN THIS BOOK, YOU MAY MISS SOME OF THE USEFUL INFORMATION THAT I HAVE INCLUDED FOR PARTICULAR DESIGNS, SO I HAVE DECIDED TO SUMMARIZE THE MOST IMPORTANT POINTS HERE.

1. PATTERNS

You might find it difficult with some of the projects to get the patterns to fit the wood or to line up as you wish. If this is the case, you can do some of the early roughing out without a pattern and then draw it on later – see the diving kingfisher on pages 132–9.

With some projects, a pattern is not even necessary. Sometimes you just have to have an idea and let it develop, especially if there is a risk of pieces breaking. If you are too rigid with your design, it becomes impossible to adjust when things go wrong (and they very often do!).

2. CUTTING OUT

I have a band saw, so cutting out patterns is not difficult for me, but I appreciate that most readers will only have basic equipment. A coping saw can be useful for small areas but is not always suitable for making long cuts. As an alternative, you can draw straight lines from the edge of the block to the drawn pattern, as close together as you wish, all around the drawn outline. You then cut along these lines with a normal tenon saw or similar. Once this is done you can chip out the waste between the lines with a chisel or knife.

3. KEEPING THE TOOLS SHARP

As nearly all of these projects are going to take a little time to finish, you are certainly going to need to sharpen your tools once or twice during the process. In general, I recommend that you hone or strop your knife or gouge at least every half an hour or so of use. You may not notice that your tools are getting blunt, only that the quality of your cuts gets worse and the amount of effort you use becomes greater. Once your tools lose their sharp edge, you are far more likely to get breakages to your work and cuts to your hands. See pages 16–17 for advice on sharpening.

4. OBTAINING THE BASIC SHAPE

The biggest problem when woodcarving or whittling is not really anything to do with actually removing wood, it is more about constant looking and seeing exactly WHERE the wood needs to be removed.

If you don't know enough about your subject and cannot recognize where all its components should be placed, you have no chance of carving it accurately. As a result, the biggest part of the process is to establish the location of the various parts. The overall shape can be achieved at the roughing-out stage and this should be enough for you to recognize exactly what the carving is supposed to be. What detail you add is up to you and should enhance the shape and increase what character the figure already has.

It is at this stage that you might need to make any adjustments to your original design to make sure that you can actually carve it. I very often find that there are areas that I cannot reach with a tool and that I need to change things slightly to be able to gain access. If this is not done at this stage you may end up with some very untidy parts to your finished carving.

5. COLOUR

Adding colour to a carving is something that is very common in the USA but has been resisted by carvers in the UK for centuries. In spite of the fact that most buildings and statues would have been brightly painted at one time, there is a definite reluctance to do much more than add oil, varnish or wax polish to a finished piece.

There are many different ways to add colour to a carving: you can paint, stain or dye a piece very easily with products readily available. In addition, Procion dyes, which are used for fabric work, can be used very effectively on wood without the risk of the dye bleeding into areas where it is not wanted. This was used to colour the rocks under the octopus (see pages 116–23).

A useful way of adding a grey, brown or even black colour is to treat the wood with a solution made by soaking steel wool (or a nail) in vinegar or cola for a day or two. When added to the wood, this reacts with the tannin in the wood and will change its colour to grey or brown. By adding more tannin (by dabbing with a wet tea bag), you can make the brown darker or even turn it to a black. You will need to test the process on a spare piece of the same wood as the results will change from wood to wood. The beaver (see pages 110–15) has been coloured this way.

If you want to paint your work, I suggest that you first do so with very diluted paint and then add any further colour if needed. Using a solid colour can totally obliterate the wood grain, which is why many people don't like the process. The pelican (see pages 66–71) was painted using this method.

7. AVOIDING DAMAGE

There are problems that the whittler will have that the normal carver doesn't need to worry about. This is because the carving is held in the hand and there is always the possibility of breakage due to crushing. Apart from being aware of this, there are precautions that you can take. Make sure that, during the carving process, you keep all delicate areas supported by some other part of the carving, to be released when the bulk of the work has been completed. Also, try to hold the piece by a secure part and protect the delicate areas as much as you can. Complete the 'heavier' parts of the carving first and leave the finer parts until the end. If you have the luxury of using something like a power rotary tool you can reduce the risk considerably.

8. BASIC DESIGN CONSIDERATIONS

Look at your design carefully before you do any cutting out. If the subject has fine fingers, toes or claws, make sure that you can carve them without breakage and that they will be strong enough to survive. If they are not supported, it is very unlikely that they will be there for long. You really need to give them something to rest upon – a rock, leaf, branch or something similar. You could even hide them in long grass. If there is no other option than to have the delicate parts exposed (a bird's beak, for example), strengthen the delicate piece by adding a few coats of cyanoacrylate glue (superglue). Do this outside as the glue's fumes can be toxic.

When you eventually get to the point where you are adding the fine detail, make sure that your tools are extra sharp and that you can actually see what it is that you want to add. Almost certainly, any figures or animals that you are carving will initially be slightly larger or fatter than you really want. You must remember that there is rarely any indication of size or scale with sculptures of any kind so the slimmer you make your carving, the taller it will appear to be. As a result, much of the detailing work will involve removing bulk, adding eyes, fur or feathers (if required) and toes or claws, etc.

9. ADDING EYES

All the subjects in this book have eyes, and carving these can cause quite a bit of heartache and frighten many carvers, beginners and experienced alike, especially as the eyes are generally very small. You will need to check if the creature has shaped or round eyes. If they are round, you can carve the outline with an appropriately sized gouge and then either shape the eye, drill and insert a piece of contrasting timber or horn, or add a glass eye that can be obtained easily from online suppliers. If the animal's eyes are shaped, you have little alternative but to carve the shape using a very small gouge, chisel or knife.

Whatever shape the eye is, if you choose to carve the eye, you can paint it an appropriate colour, usually black, and apply a tiny drop of clear nail varnish, which will give it a sparkling finish. I have found this to be the most effective way of producing realistic small eyes. Just adding glass eyes to any random creature can very easily spoil all the effort you have put in as most eyes also have eyelids which cannot be carved with glass eyes. The section on dealing with eyes will show you the different techniques available (see pages 22–7). I have used almost all of these methods in the different projects in this book.

10. WHEN THINGS GO WRONG

I don't think I have ever carved something where nothing at all has gone wrong, but then I am always trying something new or different and am never really sure how a carving is going to turn out. That is the fun of it for me. 'Safe' carving has never really appealed to me. Even if you prefer to be safe, wood can be unpredictable and things can still go wrong. The usual reaction, when this happens, is to worry about what you did wrong and how to put it right. It could well be that you didn't do anything wrong and, anyway it doesn't matter as it is already done.

The solution to all problems is the same – take off more wood – unless you like gluing bits back on, something I only do if there is absolutely no alternative.

I have to admit that, when I need to change a carving because of a mistake, it generally turns out better than it would have been otherwise. So stop worrying about where you went wrong, and instead try to work out where the wood has to be taken off to fix it. By carefully checking and finishing, your work will look superb!

Getting started

IN ALL OF THE PROJECTS I HAVE INCLUDED ONE OR TWO DRAWN PATTERNS TO GET YOU STARTED. THESE WILL NEED TO BE COPIED OR TRACED AT THE SIZE YOU WANT YOUR CARVING TO BE. THIS CAN BE DONE ON A PRINTER OR ENLARGED BY DRAWING ON SQUARED PAPER AND REDRAWN WITH BIGGER SQUARES.

The best way to use these patterns is to cut them out of stiff card so they don't get distorted when they're drawn onto the block. These patterns do not generally show any of the detail you will need to complete the carving but this can be taken from reference photos as you go along, either of the finished piece or from your own research on the particular animal.

USING THE PATTERNS

To begin, I suggest that you draw one pattern on your block and shade in the waste to be removed. If you draw both patterns at once you will lose one as soon as you start cutting out unless you are very careful.

Draw the first pattern on the block and shade in the waste.

After cutting out the waste, you will be left with a squared block roughly following the outlines of your patterns.

Remove all the waste you have shaded, then draw the second pattern on the cut areas. While doing this, don't hold the pattern flat against the cut surface. Copy it as if it were in the original position on the flat block. Again, it is important that the patterns are the right way round and are level at the top and bottom. Shade the waste as before and remove the shaded areas. You will now have a squared block corresponding with the outlines of your patterns. In some cases, the patterns may be side and top; if so, deal with only one view at a time. This is the easy bit.

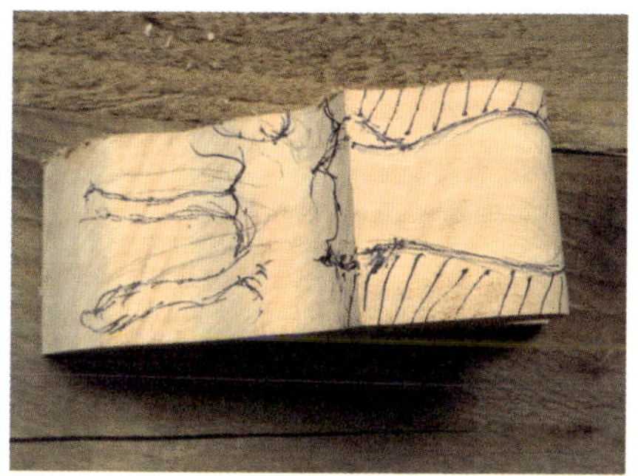

Draw and redraw the details of the animal as you carve.

From now on you will need to draw and redraw the details as you carve, using the patterns and the pictures of the process as your references. In addition, any pictures or photographs that you may have of the subject will obviously be of help. If you are confident, you can modify the detail as you go along, even changing the pose or, in some cases, the actual animal. Anything needed should be included in the individual project instructions.

TACKLING THE PROJECTS

The projects get increasingly more complicated as you progress through the book and, in most cases, there are additional skills and learning points to take on board. This doesn't mean that you have to attempt them in the correct order but you will pick up different things as you go along.

The carving process for these projects is not all that difficult. The biggest problem is establishing where everything is within the piece of wood. Part of this is a sound knowledge of your subject, but the rest is largely trial and error. I tend to draw a lot on my carvings until I am sure where I am going. Often this is very different from what I originally intended. Don't be afraid to follow a diversion if you come to a halt. Rather like encountering a roadblock on a car journey, you will still get there but by a different route.

Just remember, unlike with painting pictures, you cannot easily hide anything or 'suggest' a detail. You have to know what it is you are carving, so don't plough on if you are not sure what you are hoping to achieve. If you are not sure, stop and check the instructions, the internet or another carving book.

What is most important is to get the basic form and spirit of the subject before you try to add any fine detail. Imagine your carving as a simple outline or shadow – is it recognizable? If so, continue. If not, change it. On this point I would give you a small piece of advice. It is not easy to capture the 'essence' of the subject. By that I mean what makes you recognize the subject for what it is and what its nature is likely to be. If, during the carving process, your piece takes on the appearance of a different animal, I would be inclined to go with it as you may never get back on course and you will lose what you already have. If your beaver looks more like an otter, why not stick with it rather than fight the wood? You are not very likely to win that battle!

KNOW WHEN TO STOP

You need to decide how far you want to go with the subject. If you haven't done much carving, I suggest that you keep it simple. If your finished carving is recognizable as the animal it is intended to be, leave it at that. Many carvings I have seen have been spoilt by going just that bit too far.

Once you have experience you can start to be a little more ambitious by increasing the amount of detail like adding inlaid eyes, texturing the fur and so on. Remember, though, that you need to know how the fur runs on an animal if you are to get it right. In general, the hair tracts on nearly all animals are pretty similar so you don't have a huge amount to remember. It usually parts down the centre of the body running backwards and down. It runs down and backwards on the legs on four-legged animals but on two-legged ones it runs down the upper arm but across the lower arm. On the head it runs down and back on the muzzle, round the eyes and back and down on the forehead. For some reason, the hair on the nose of cats goes forward.

There is one more small point that is worth remembering. These projects are mostly carved from basswood that is 1⅛in (30mm) or 1⅝in (40mm) square in section and 6in (150mm) long. This means that the poses are limited to what will fit into this block. There is nothing to stop you adjusting the final pose by mounting the figure at an angle to make it look more natural or even adding it to another piece of wood. I have done this with the dolphins (see pages 60–65) and the otter (see pages 102–109) and I think the results are an improvement on the original carving. Also, don't forget that you can fill and paint a carving if you have any problems such as flaws or splits in the wood (or unintentional design modifications that you didn't really want).

Finally, as I mentioned in the introduction, this is only a piece of wood. If you go wrong, you can start again. The answer to any problem that you may encounter is to take off more wood – you just have to decide where you need to do this. And there are some very good glues about nowadays if you need to stick some wood back on! But above all, enjoy yourself.

Projects

Duck

WHEREVER YOU LIVE, YOU WILL NOT BE FAR FROM A RIVER, POND OR LAKE, SO YOU WILL HAVE PLENTY OF OPPORTUNITY TO STUDY DUCKS IN ALL KINDS OF POSES. THE ONE I HAVE CHOSEN IS A FAIRLY TYPICAL POSE OF A DUCK SNOOZING ON THE BANK. IT'S A VERY SIMPLE PATTERN SO YOU CAN FOLLOW THIS ONE OR MAKE UP ONE OF YOUR OWN BASED ON YOUR RESEARCH. THE WHITTLING PROCESS WILL BE THE SAME WHATEVER THE POSE, BUT YOU MIGHT PREFER TO HAVE A CARVING THAT IS YOUR OWN DESIGN AND, THEREFORE, UNIQUE TO YOU.

TOOLBOX

- Basswood block, 1⅛ x 1⅛ x 2⅜in (30 x 30 x 60mm), or whatever size you wish
- Pencil
- Paper or card
- Safety glove
- Band saw or coping saw
- Knife
- Abrasives
- Finishing oil or wax polish

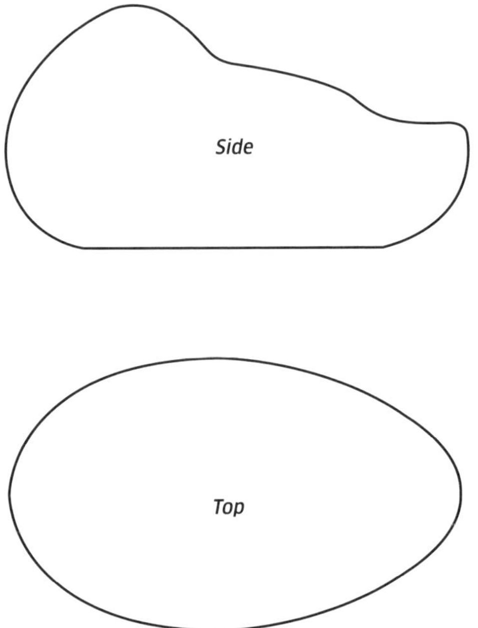

Templates to scale: copy at 100%

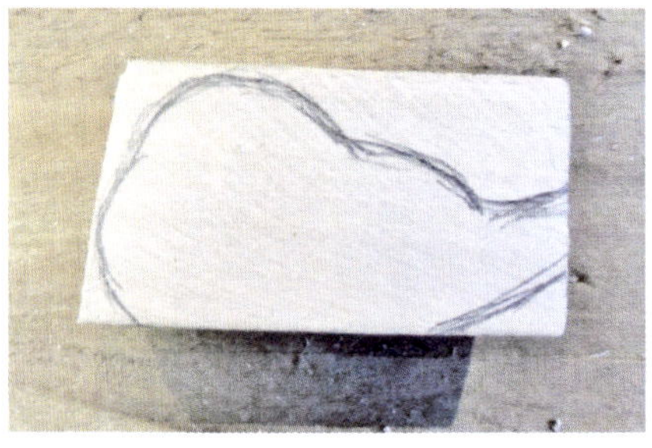

1 You may find it useful to copy the pattern onto card or paper first. Then, copy the side pattern onto your basswood block in pencil.

2 Next, line up the top pattern and copy that onto the top of your block. Mark out the waste as shown.

3 Cut out the outlines of the duck using a band saw or coping saw, then draw in the area where the head will be. The rest of the carving can be achieved using just your knife.

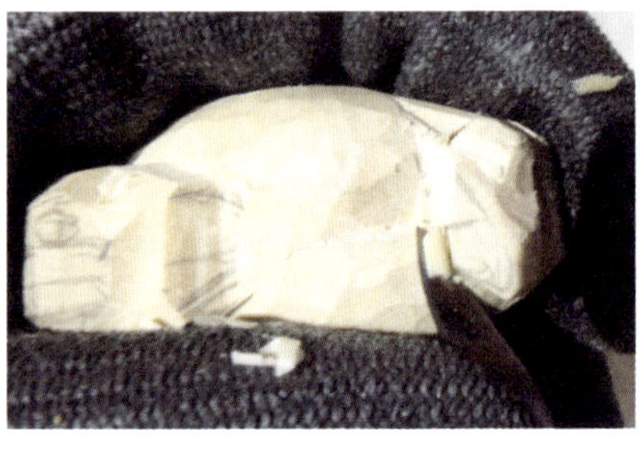

4 The wood can seem shapeless at this stage. Spend time locating the important parts: head, wings, tail etc.

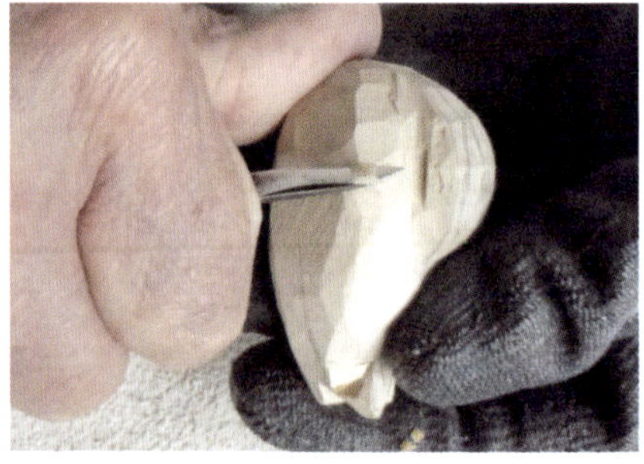

5 Round off the body, cutting round the outline of the head.

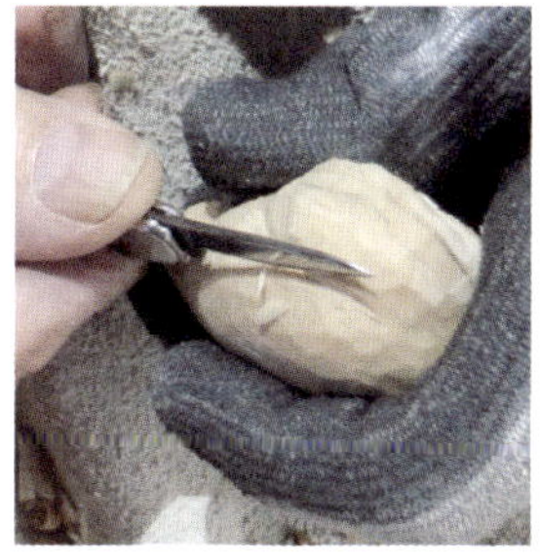

6 Now begin to shape the duck's head by cutting down each side.

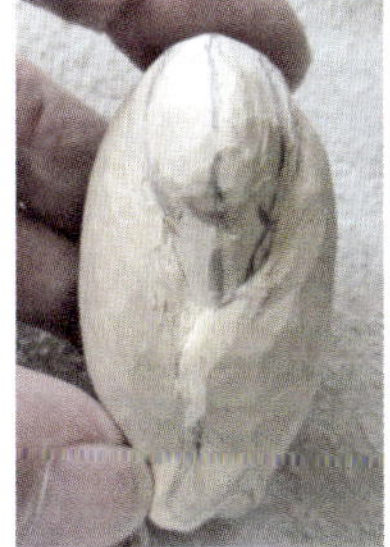

7 Roughly define the beak and wings. If you're following my pattern, the duck's beak should be tucked slightly under one wing.

8 Now that you've got all the main elements in the right places, it's time to clean up the whole shape and get rid of any 'fuzzy' areas or pencil marks that have been left behind. As the duck is asleep in my design, you don't need to worry about carving the eyes. (If you've chosen a different design that does include open eyes, see pages 22–7 for advice on adding eyes.)

9 To finish, you can either sand the carving or leave the tool marks as they are. Add a coat of finishing oil or wax polish and then your duck is complete.

Heron

WE HAVE A LARGE POND IN OUR GARDEN IN WHICH I PLACED A FEW FISH SEVERAL YEARS AGO TO HELP KEEP DOWN THE MOSQUITOES. AS DUCKS AND OTHER WILDLIFE FOUND THE POND, THE FISH POPULATION EXPLODED. HOWEVER, THIS WAS SOON DISCOVERED BY THE LOCAL HERONS. ALTHOUGH THE FISH POPULATION HAS DECREASED SINCE THEY ARRIVED, THERE ARE STILL SHOALS OF VERY SMALL FRY APPEARING ON A REGULAR BASIS, SO WE CONTINUE TO ENJOY THE SIGHT OF THE HERONS FROM TIME TO TIME. WE DON'T HAVE ANY EXOTIC FISH – THEY ARE ALL NATURAL ENGLISH RIVER FISH, SO THEY ARE ONLY TAKING THE SAME CHANCES THAT THEY DO NATURALLY (EXCEPT THAT WE FEED THEM!)

The pose I have chosen for this project is slightly stylized and more typical of when herons are hiding rather than when they are hunting.

TOOLBOX

- Basswood block, 1⅝ x 1⅝ x 6in (40 x 40 x 150mm), or whatever size you wish
- Pencil
- Paper or card
- Safety glove
- Band saw or coping saw
- Knife
- Small gouge
- V-tool
- Abrasives (optional)
- Finishing oil or wax polish
- Pin
- Block of wood in contrasting colour

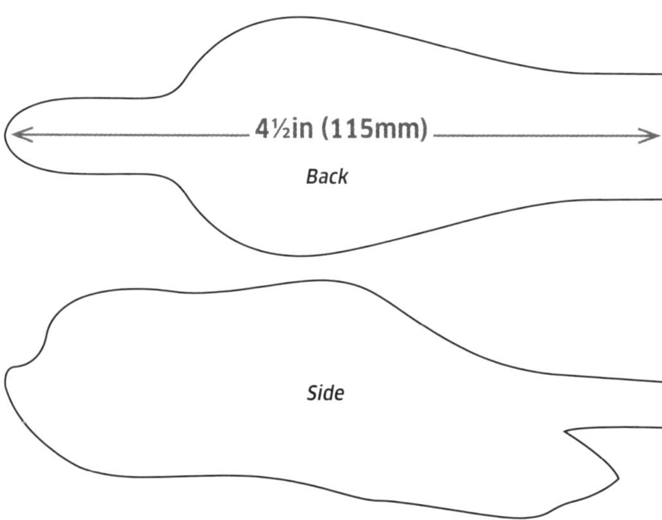

Templates not to scale: copy at 120%

1 Start by marking out the patterns, making sure that they line up with each other. This shows my original sketch but the patterns will give you the same result.

2 Your marks don't have to be too detailed at this stage, just enough to see what waste needs to be removed around the heron shape. I have left a square base at the bottom of the block to hold onto while carving; the heron will be cut off from this when the carving is finished.

3 Cut out the outlines you have marked using a band saw or coping saw.

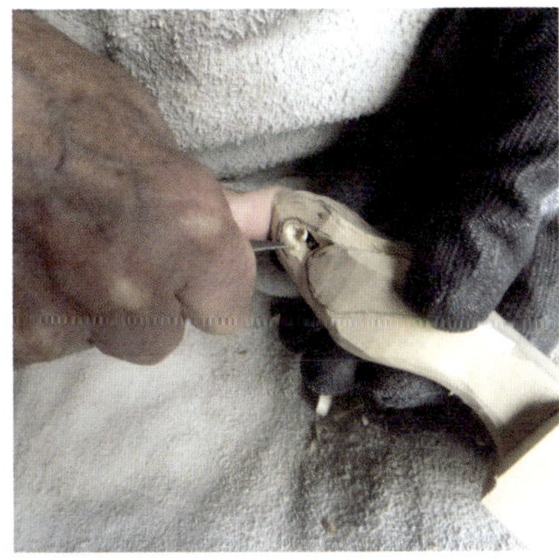

5 Using your knife or a small gouge, tidy up the gap under the neck.

4 Use your knife to roughly round off the body, marking in the areas to be carved later, i.e. the wings, head, etc. Carefully cut through the area under the neck, making sure that the body, head and neck on each side match up with each other.

6 Then cut away the waste wood on the shoulders to shape the head.

7 Mark in the tail area and remove the waste so that you can finish shaping the body.

8 Re-draw the detail on the head and wings, checking that any lines you have drawn are the same on each side.

9 Continue rounding off the body and head using a combination of the knife, gouge and V-tool until you are happy with the overall shape. Don't worry too much about the finish and detail at this stage as it is the basic shape that is most important.

10 Once you're happy with the shape, go over the whole carving and make sure all your cuts are clean and the surface is smooth. You can, of course, sand the whole piece but this will add considerably more work and I think this piece looks better showing the result of the cuts you have made as long as they are neat.

11 The final task is to add the eyes. You can leave them as small slits for closed eyes, you can insert an eye or you can carve it (see pages 22–7 for more details). I chose to carve the eyes for my project. Add a finishing oil or wax polish. Cut the heron free from the base and fit it onto a mount of your choice; I opted for a square block in a contrasting wood, which the heron was attached to using a pin.

Cormorant

THE CORMORANT IS A BIRD THAT, PROBABLY, FEW PEOPLE EVER GET THE CHANCE TO SEE IN REAL LIFE. IN THE UK THEY TEND TO FREQUENT THE SEASHORE AND ESTUARIES, AND YOU MAY OCCASIONALLY SEE A CORMORANT OR SHAG (WHICH HAS A SLIGHTLY DIFFERENT SHAPE) AS THEY SEARCH FOR FISH. IN PARTS OF THE USA ANOTHER VARIATION, THE ANHINGA OR SNAKE BIRD, IS VERY COMMON IN STATES SUCH AS FLORIDA, WHILE THE CORMORANT IS STILL USED FOR FISHING IN ASIA.

When at rest they are typically seen with wings spread as they dry out after periods in the water. They are certainly birds with very obvious attitude, and I have tried to show this in this project.

TOOLBOX

- Basswood block, 6 x 1⅛ x 1⅛in (150 x 30 x 30mm); you may find this design easier to carve from a slightly larger piece
- Pencil
- Paper or card
- Safety glove
- Knife
- Wax polish

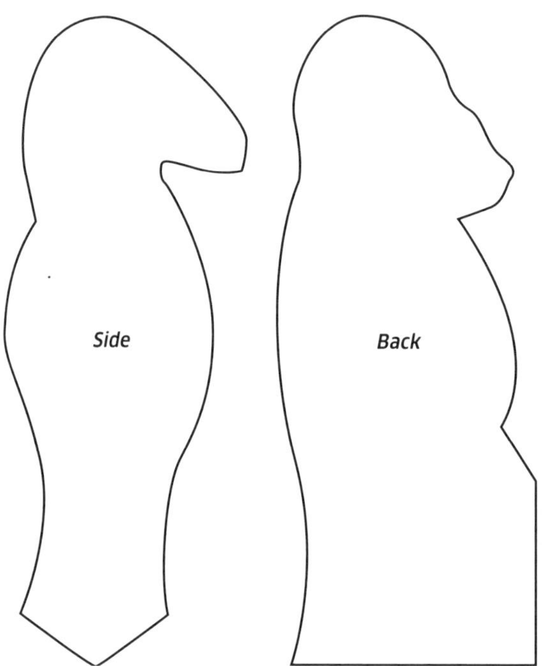

Templates to scale: copy at 100%

1 Draw both patterns onto your block making sure that they are the right way round. Do not cut away any of the waste at this stage as the wood at the bottom will be the rock on which the bird sits.

2 Mark the angle of the head and beak on the top of the block, allowing yourself plenty of wood for the beak (see Tip on page 53).

3 Use your knife to trim off the waste around this area down to about ¾in (20mm) from the top.

4 Round off the shoulders and shape the twist of the neck and head. Leave the beak shaping until later.

5 You can now start to shape the back and front of the body, drawing in the detail you intend to include as you go.

6 You should now have all the elements more or less in place so you can start to refine and add the detail. I usually draw all over the carving at this stage to make sure that I don't miss anything and that everything is where it should be. I don't want to carve anything until I am sure it is what I want and where I have decided it should be.

7 I decided to carve a simple eye on this piece but you can either paint the eyes or insert a piece of contrasting material if you prefer (see pages 22–7 for advice on adding eyes). Once you have carved the eye you can thin down the beak. This is very characteristic of the cormorant so you will need to look at reference pictures of the bird or carefully follow the photos in this project.

8 I gave the front of the bird a light texture and carved some simple feathers.

9 As a finishing touch, I added some texture to the base of the block to make it look like a rock. I don't think this piece would be improved by sanding so have just given it a couple of coats of wax polish.

TIP

With a bird that has a very long thin beak like this, leave plenty of wood and do not thin down until the majority of the carving is complete. This will decrease the likelihood of breaking the beak while carving.

Albatross

THE WANDERING ALBATROSS AND OTHER MEMBERS OF THE ALBATROSS FAMILY HAVE THE LONGEST WINGSPAN OF ANY BIRD. THEY SPEND MOST OF THEIR LIVES IN THE AIR, ONLY LANDING TO FEED OR BREED. ONE BIRD WAS RECORDED AS FLYING AROUND 3,700 MILES (5,950KM) IN 12 DAYS. THEY ARE FOUND MOSTLY IN THE SOUTHERN HEMISPHERE AND ARE ENDANGERED. I HAVE INCLUDED THIS AS A PROJECT AS I HAVE NEVER SEEN ONE AND SUSPECT THAT MANY READERS WON'T HAVE DONE SO EITHER.

TOOLBOX

- Basswood block, 1⅝ x 1⅝ x 6in (40 x 40 x 150mm), or whatever size you wish
- Pencil
- Paper or card
- Safety glove
- Knife
- Abrasives
- Cyanoacrylate glue (optional)
- Finishing oil or wax polish
- Pin
- Block in contrasting wood

They are incredibly graceful birds and lend themselves to being a subject for a carving. There is not much detail to include and the bird can be mounted in any way that shows off its form well. The whole piece can be completed using only a knife.

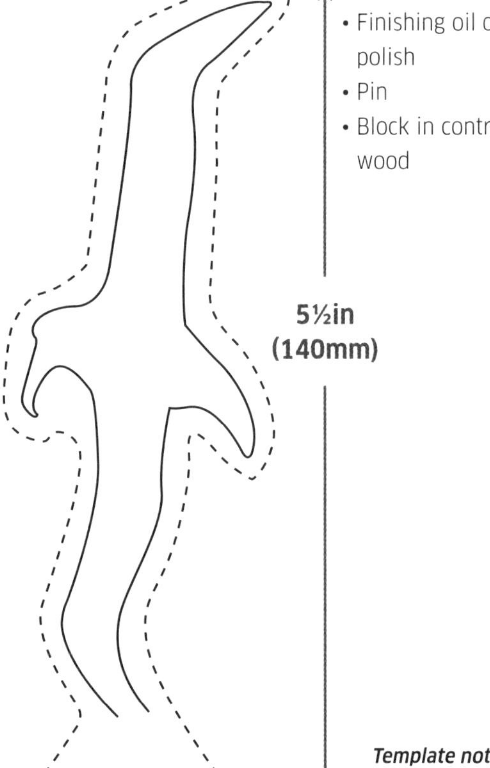

Template not to scale: copy at 123%

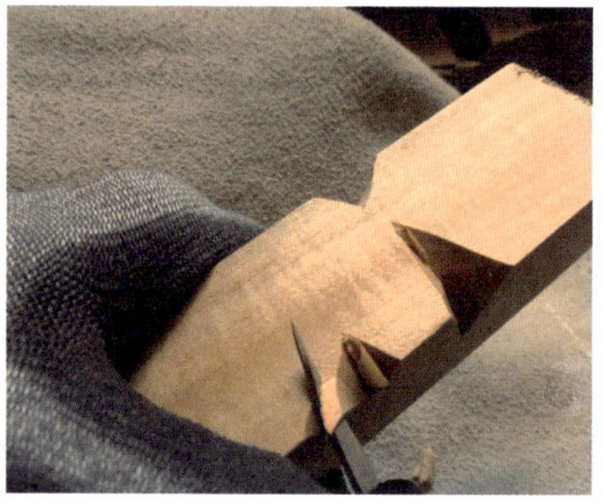

1 I decided to place the body of the bird diagonally on my basswood block to maximize the length. This does make using a pattern rather difficult initially, so I suggest you cut out the pattern from a piece of card for future reference and, once you have flattened off some of the corners, draw a rough outline (as shown by the dotted lines) for the initial roughing out. Find the centre point in the length of the block and leave an area about $\frac{9}{16}$in (15mm) either side of this point. Using your knife, make a wedge cut on each edge to define this area, which will be the body.

2 Take the corners off two opposite sides along the length from the middle to one end. Repeat at the other end and mark in where you think the wings and body of the albatross will be.

3 Cut out the outlines of the wings and body and start to slim down the wings to give an idea of the shape you want them to be.

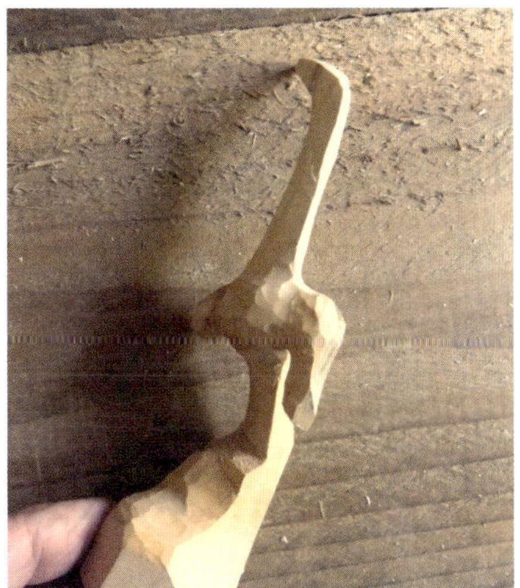

4 Narrow down the wings and give a preliminary shape to the body and head. You can make the top wing as thin as you like but keep a bit of thickness on the lower wing to give it some strength as you carve. You should be able to use your cardboard cutout for this.

5 Leaving the beak thick for strength, continue to slim down the wings to the base. You will need to leave the base attached to allow you to display the bird in an attractive flying position.

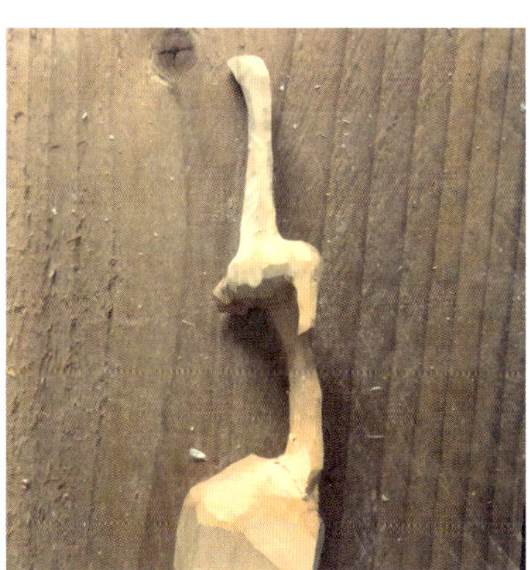

6 The main shapes should now be correct and everything should be where you need it to be, so you can start to add detail to the body and head.

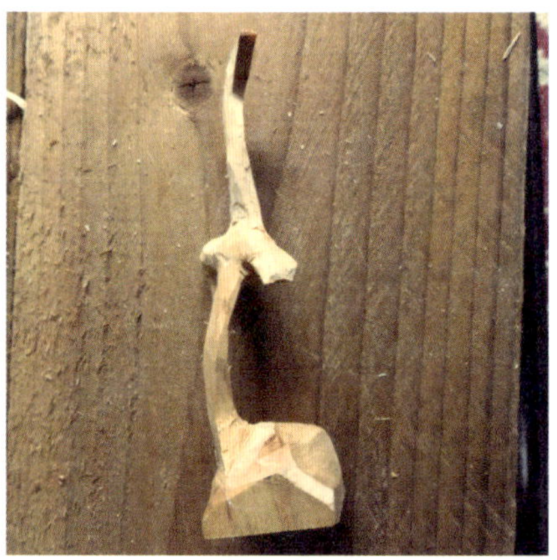

7 As you add detail, continue to shape the wings where necessary.

8 You can now adjust the angle of the carving and finish the beak. To look natural, the bird needs to be positioned so that its beak is vertical. This may mean that you need to chamfer some wood off part of the underside of the base to get it to sit right.

9 Give the whole carving a gentle sanding as I think this subject looks better when it is smooth. If you want your tool marks to be visible, that is fine, you can just skip this stage.

TIP

A carving of this size is too small to consider adding or inserting eyes, so I would not recommend attempting it. Realistic eyes are also not required on stylized pieces like this.

10 As well as giving a smoother appearance, sanding also allows you to slim down the wings even further, if necessary, until you have the fineness you want. Be careful, though, as the piece will now be very delicate. If you are worried about the delicacy of the beak, you can give it a few coats of cyanoacrylate (superglue) as this will harden the wood considerably, making it less vulnerable.

11 Give the whole piece a couple of coats of finishing oil or wax polish.

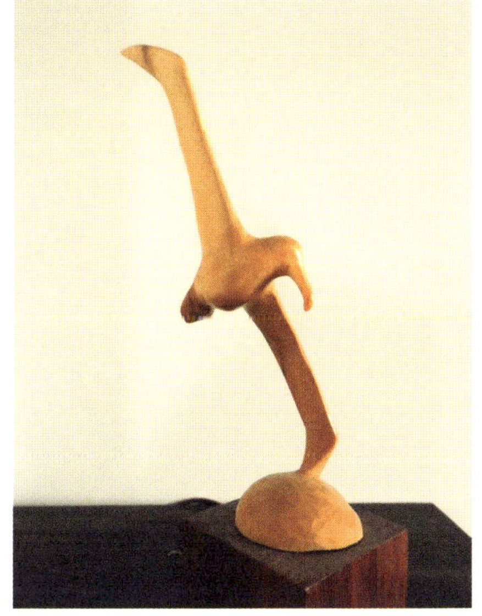

12 You can leave the albatross as it is or mount it on a contrasting wooden block to give it more stability. The size of the mount is up to you; it just needs to be big enough to keep the carving stable.

Dolphins

ONE OF THE FIRST SUBJECTS THAT MANY NEW WOODCARVERS ATTEMPT IS THE DOLPHIN IN ONE FORM OR ANOTHER. I THINK THIS IS BECAUSE IT IS A PLEASING SHAPE WITH VERY FEW DIFFICULT AREAS AND, WHEN THE CARVING IS FINISHED, IT LOOKS GOOD ON DISPLAY. HOWEVER, THIS DOESN'T MEAN THAT IT'S THAT EASY TO GET RIGHT – MANY EXAMPLES THAT I HAVE SEEN HAVE HAD SOME SERIOUS ERRORS! IT IS IMPORTANT TO CHECK YOUR WORK AGAINST PICTURES OF DOLPHINS, ESPECIALLY AS THERE ARE VARIATIONS BETWEEN THE DIFFERENT TYPES.

Before you start whittling, think about how you intend to display the dolphin – will it be swimming or leaping? And will it be attached to a mount? These choices will affect the tail position, so you might have to alter this from the pattern I've supplied.

TOOLBOX

- Basswood block, 1⅛ x 1⅛ x 2⅜in (30 x 30 x 60mm), or whatever size you wish
- Pencil
- Paper or card
- Safety glove
- Knife
- Abrasives
- Finishing oil or wax polish
- Pins (optional)
- Driftwood base (optional)

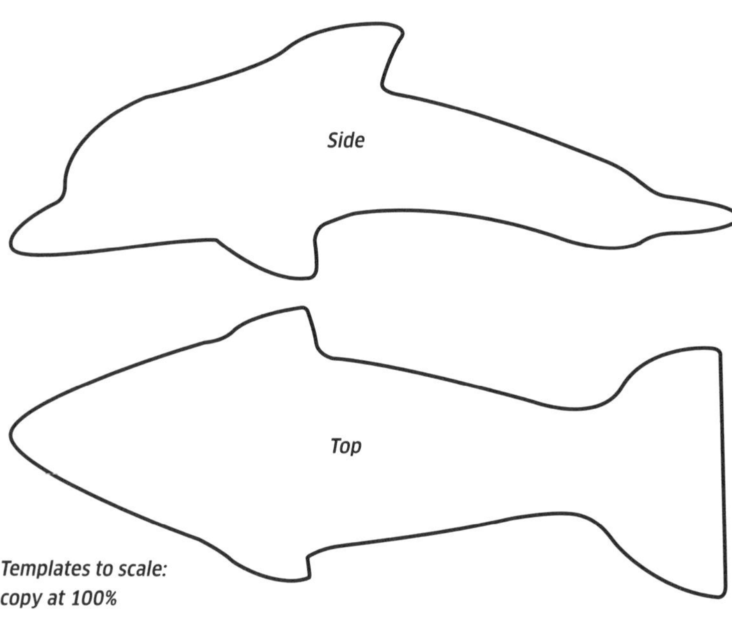

Templates to scale: copy at 100%

1 My dolphin design has fins sticking out on each side so I decided to carve it on a diagonal; this meant it was not possible to draw the pattern onto the block. In this case, I suggest that you make a card or paper cutout of the top pattern and draw the outline roughly over one long edge of the block in order to define the waste to be removed.

2 The waste wood can be removed using just your knife on this project. You will find it easiest to begin by making a V cut on each side of each fin and the tail.

3 Once you have done this on each side it should be fairly easy to remove the waste by cutting between the V cuts. Allow the grain to split as this will help with the cutting.

4 Trim the wood as neatly as you can, making sure that the sides match.

5 You can now draw on the side view and then remove the waste as marked with your knife.

6 At this point, you should have a squared-off dolphin shape, which you can now start to round off.

7 These mammals are extremely streamlined so make sure that there are no square or flat surfaces left on the body, head or tail. Refer to photographs of your chosen species to help you get the lines correct.

TIP

This is a fairly quick carving to complete so I think it is worth making more than one dolphin, as I did, and mounting them together to make a more interesting display.

8 As you have only used a knife for the carving, you will probably have some ragged areas that need to be removed so give the whole piece a thorough sanding. Then remove it from the spare wood and finish shaping the tail. Remember that a dolphin's tail is horizontal, not vertical like a fish. As this is a fairly basic carving, you don't need to include eyes; however, if you do wish to add them, a couple of simple carved lines will suffice.

9 The way you mount your dolphin will depend on whether you want it to be leaping upwards or forwards. I decided that, as I had carved two dolphins, I would mount them as a pair leaping forwards. You may have to experiment a bit with the size and shape of the base to ensure that it is stable. For my project, I used a piece of driftwood and secured the dolphins using pins.

10 Finally, add the finishing oil or wax polish of your choice to complete the project.

Pelican

IF YOU ARE EVER FORTUNATE ENOUGH TO VISIT COASTAL AREAS OR WATERWAYS IN THE TROPICS, YOU WILL ALMOST CERTAINLY ENCOUNTER THE PELICAN IN ITS NATURAL HABITAT. IT APPEARS TO BE QUITE AN UNGAINLY BIRD BUT AS SOON AS IT TAKES TO THE AIR OVER THE WATER ON ONE OF ITS MANY FISHING TRIPS, IT TAKES ON THE APPEARANCE OF A WORLD WAR II LOW-FLYING BOMBER. AS SOON AS IT SEES FISH IT DISAPPEARS SUDDENLY IN A MASS OF SPRAY AS IT DIVES TO CATCH ITS LUNCH, ONLY TO EXPLODE OUT OF THE WATER MOMENTS LATER WITH ITS POUCH BULGING WITH FISH. OTHER PELICANS EITHER JOIN IN OR SIT ON CONVENIENT POSTS TO WATCH THE SHOW.

It is this watching pose that I have chosen for this project. However, as the pose did not fit on the wood I had available, I used a piece of spare wood for the post and fixed the two together with a small pin.

TOOLBOX

- Basswood block, 1⅝ x 1⅝ x 6in (40 x 40 x 150mm), or whatever size you wish
- Pencil
- Paper or card
- Safety glove
- Coping saw or other small saw
- Knife
- Selection of small palm gouges
- V-tool
- Brown acrylic paint (optional)
- Finishing oil or wax polish
- Black acrylic paint (optional)
- Small pin (optional)

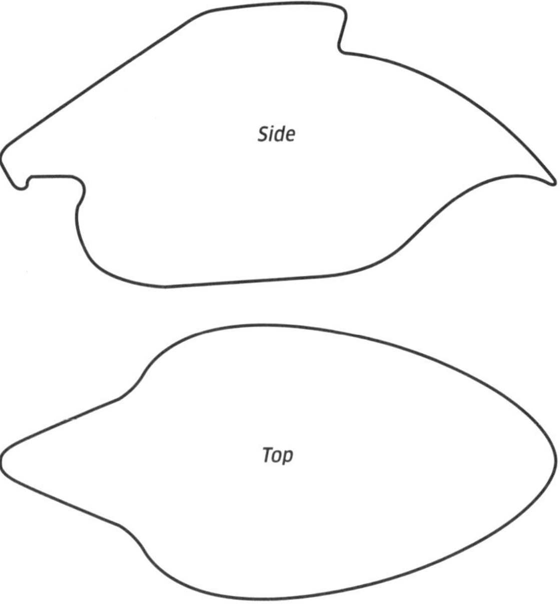

Templates to scale: copy at 100%

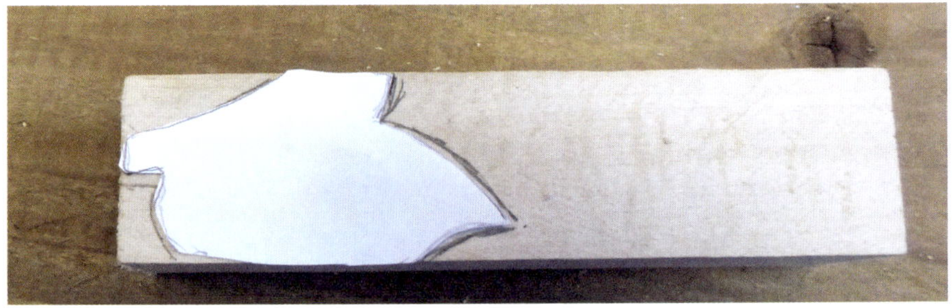

1 Draw the pattern of the side view onto your block.

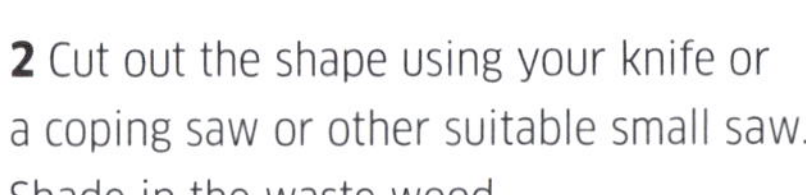

2 Cut out the shape using your knife or a coping saw or other suitable small saw. Shade in the waste wood.

3 Remove the waste wood that you have marked using your knife and draw on the head and beak shapes, shading in the wood you need to remove.

4 Remove this waste wood from either side of the head using your knife.

5 This should leave the shape of the pelican's head clearly defined.

6 Round off the body and wing area, leaving further shaping of the head until later.

7 Next, use a selection of small gouges to define the wings and create a small lower area at the back, between the wings, for the bird's body and tail.

8 You can now shape the head and beak using a combination of the knife and gouges. I suggest that you refer to some clear photographs of a pelican's head to get this right, as I did. What you think is there may well not be the case, so it is better to check.

9 Mark some lines on the wings to represent the feathers. The more random you make this the better – avoid straight lines. For the eyes, you can draw or paint them, inlay a piece of contrasting wood or do what I did – show the bird with its eyes closed.

10 Cut these lines on the wings with a small V-tool to complete the carving work.

11 I chose to give the whole piece a light coat of paint but if you prefer to leave it a natural wood colour, give it a couple of coats of finishing oil or wax polish. For the final touch, I mounted the pelican on a post made from an offcut of the basswood block. To add some realism, I carved a ring on the post and painted it black to represent a boat-mooring ring. The bird was secured to the post by a small pin.

TIP

The block of basswood I used was slightly longer than I needed for this piece, but the extra length provided something to hold while carving. An offcut from the block came in handy for the post that the finished bird is attached to.

Courting grebes

THERE ARE 22 VARIETIES OF GREBE; PROBABLY THE MOST COMMON ARE THE GREAT CRESTED GREBES (UK), AND THE WESTERN GREBES (NORTH AMERICA). THEY BOTH HAVE LONG, SLENDER NECKS AND THIN DAGGER-LIKE BEAKS. WHAT MAKES THEM STAND OUT FROM OTHER WATER BIRDS IS THEIR SPECTACULAR COURTING RITUALS, WHERE THEY RISE UP AND RACE ACROSS THE SURFACE OF THE WATER, BRINGING GIFTS TO EACH OTHER AND PERFORMING ELABORATE DISPLAYS.

I have chosen to carve a pair of Great Crested Grebes. Both carvings are essentially the same and have the same stages, but I have added some weeds to one of the birds. You will need reference material to get the details right and you can, of course, only carve one bird if you prefer.

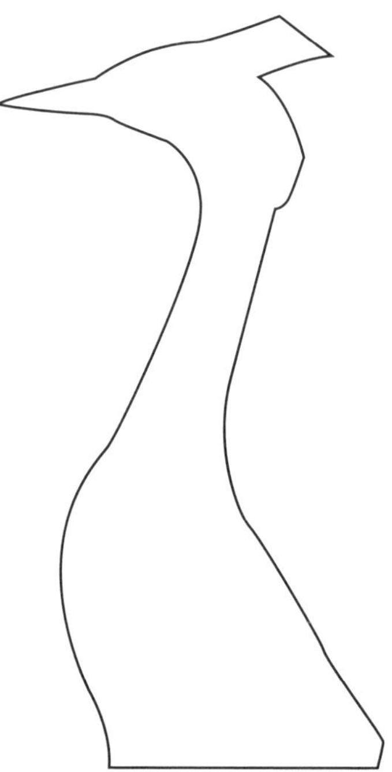

TOOLBOX

- Basswood block, 1⅝ x 1⅝ x 3½in (40 x 40 x 90mm), or whatever size you wish
- Pencil
- Paper or card
- Safety glove
- Band saw or coping saw
- Knife
- Cyanoacrylate glue (superglue)
- Abrasives
- Selection of small palm gouges
- Scalpel
- Drill
- ⅛in (3mm) amber coloured eyes (optional)
- Danish oil and wax polish
- Block of contrasting wood and blue acrylic (optional)
- Pins (optional)

Template to scale: copy at 100%

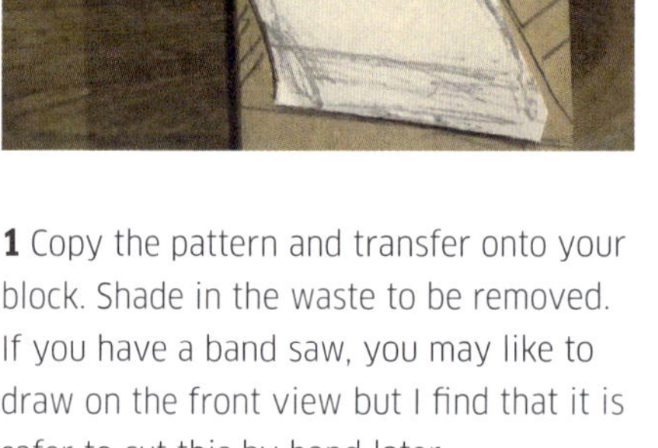

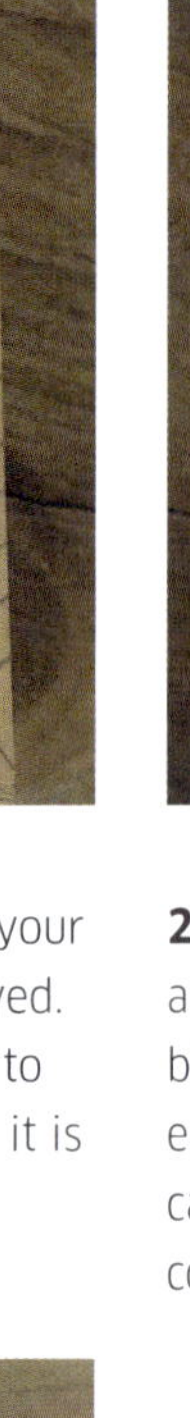

1 Copy the pattern and transfer onto your block. Shade in the waste to be removed. If you have a band saw, you may like to draw on the front view but I find that it is safer to cut this by hand later.

2 Cut out the pattern using a band saw or a coping saw. I have left it attached to the block at the bottom, not only to make it easier to hold as I carve but also so that I can adjust the angle that it will sit on once completed.

3 Now mark in the outline from the back, or front, and the angle of the head. I find that just turning the head very slightly can add a little character to a carving. If you have cut out the original pattern with a band saw, be careful not to turn the head too much as you can easily find that you don't have enough wood to complete the head. It is better to leave extra wood for the head if you intend any significant variations from the original pattern.

4 Cut away the waste using your knife, leaving plenty of wood to shape the head. These birds have crests on the top of their heads as well as all around their necks that are used to form elaborate displays. You can include these if you wish but they will make the carving rather delicate. I have left them simple.

5 You can now shape the triangle of the head at whatever angle you choose. Don't try to shape the beak yet as the grain is directly across it and you will be likely to lose much of the length. A useful procedure here to strengthen the beak is to saturate it with a very thin cyanoacrylate glue. You may need several applications, but this will make the beak very strong yet not too difficult to shape later.

6 It's a good idea to round off the body at this stage as once you detail the head, beak and neck, the whole carving becomes more delicate.

7 Sanding the body at this stage will give you a good idea of how the piece will look when it's finished.

8 It is now a matter of refining the head and adding as much detail as you wish. I think this subject would make a very attractive stylized carving and you might like to try that. I have tried to keep mine fairly realistic but without too much fine detail. Some rough sanding at this stage will give a clearer idea of the basic shape of the grebe's head.

9 Once you are happy that you have the basic overall shape, you can start to refine the head using gouges. As the beak is still a bit vulnerable, unless your knife is really sharp, I suggest that any further shaping is done with a scalpel as less pressure is needed. Just be careful not to apply too much pressure or you will snap the scalpel blade.

10 All that is now needed is to give the whole figure a thorough sanding to remove all the rough areas and previous sanding marks until a good finish is achieved.

11 I decided to fit some glass eyes at this stage and managed to get some via the internet that were the right size (see the Suppliers list on page 141). You may choose to paint the eyes or even make your own – it is up to you (see pages 22–7 for more details). All that is needed to fit glass eyes is to cut a small groove on each side of the head and drill a very small, shallow socket the diameter of the eye, about $^{3}/_{64}$in (1mm) deep so the eye can be glued in to sit more or less level with the surrounding wood. The wire at the back of the eye can be cut off or a fine hole made with a needle or very small drill into which it can be glued. All this will depend on your experience and the tools you have available.

12 Take your time when fitting the eyes to make sure they are at the same height, distance from the beak and the same depth into the head.

13 Your carving is now complete and a suitable finish can be added. I chose Danish oil and wax polish but you may prefer to use something else. I think the whole piece would look very good with a fine painted finish. I decided to display the piece with a second bird presenting some water weed, as this is very common during the grebes' courting process. The whole thing was mounted on a separate piece of wood with a small piece of blue acrylic to represent water, secured in place using glue and pins. You can, of course, choose anything you prefer to display the carvings.

TIP

If you decide to add glass eyes, I advise doing the fitting over a tray or container, as you will almost certainly drop one or both eyes and, if you do, a great deal of time will be lost while you are trying to find them. Believe me, I have been there more than once and have learnt my lesson!

Leaping fish

THERE ARE MANY WAYS OF CARVING FISH AND, ALTHOUGH THEY ARE VERY EASY TO DO, THE RESULTS CAN BE RATHER BORING AND STATIC, OFTEN REQUIRING PAINTING TO MAKE AN IMPACT. I DECIDED THAT THIS CARVING NEEDED TO SHOW A BIT OF ACTION AND I REMEMBER SITTING BY A RIVER ON ONE OCCASION WATCHING TROUT, I THINK, LEAPING OUT OF THE WATER TO CATCH FLIES. THIS PROJECT IS MY INTERPRETATION OF WHAT I SAW BUT YOU CAN ADAPT THIS HOW YOU WISH TO SUIT YOUR OWN IDEAS. THE CARVING PROCESS WILL NOT CHANGE A GREAT DEAL, WHATEVER POSE YOU CHOOSE. I HAVE ONLY INCLUDED ONE PATTERN AS THE FISH HAS A LARGE TWIST IN IT AND A SECOND PATTERN WOULDN'T HELP AT ALL.

TOOLBOX

- Basswood block, 1⅛ x1⅛ x 6in (30 x 30 x 150mm), or whatever size you wish
- Pencil
- Paper or card
- Safety glove
- Band saw or coping saw
- Knife
- Selection of small palm gouges; No.9, 3mm and No.9, 4mm are recommended
- Abrasives
- 5⁄32in (4mm) clear glass eyes (optional)
- Wax polish
- Burr or driftwood (optional)
- Pin

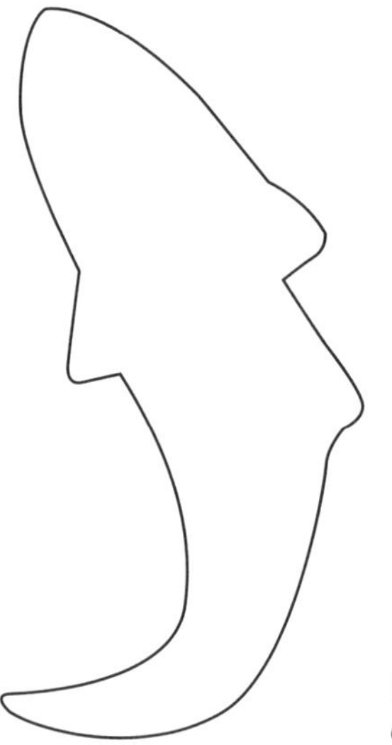

Template to scale: copy at 100%

1 Draw the pattern on to your block and mark out the waste to be removed.

2 Cut out the pattern using a band saw, a coping saw or your knife.

3 Draw a line from where the tail will be, across the edge to the centre of the side that forms the curve. This will form a line along the centre of the fish's back.

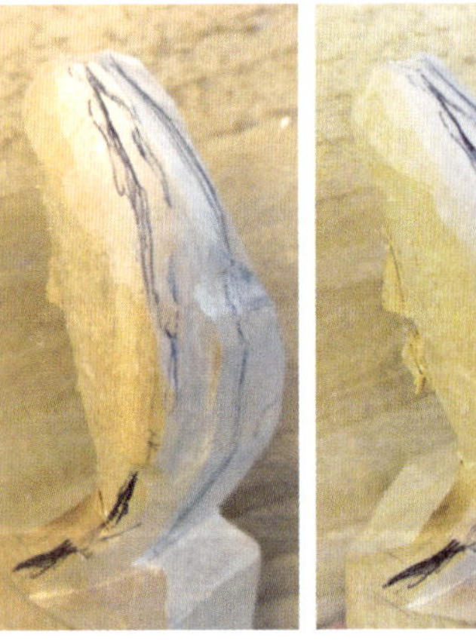

4 Mark in the fish's body around this line allowing wood for the dorsal fin. Don't touch the underside for the moment.

5 Turn to the underside and repeat the curved line representing the centre line of the fish body. Mark in and roughly shape the four main fins and allow for the small fin close to the tail. Check that the body is uniform all the way along the twist.

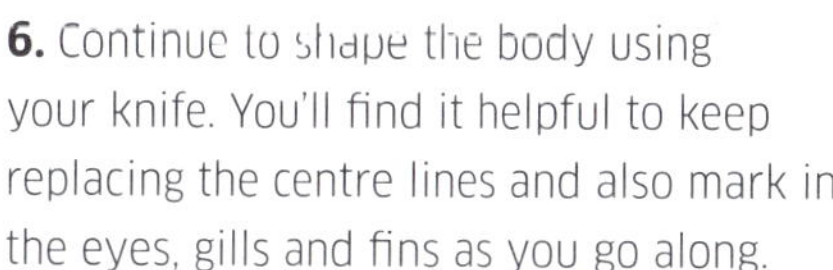

6. Continue to shape the body using your knife. You'll find it helpful to keep replacing the centre lines and also mark in the eyes, gills and fins as you go along.

7 Try to get as smooth a surface as you can as you carve as this will greatly reduce the time that you will need to sand the piece in order to get a good finish.

8 If you would prefer to mount the finished piece on a separate block, cut it off.

9 Using a small gouge, you can now shape the tail – don't make it too thin as it will be used to mount the finished fish on a new base.

10 How much detail you add is up to you; use your gouges to add the details and texture. You can leave the fish as it is, you can paint in eyes, or you can add glass eyes as I have done (see pages 22–7 for details). These were 5⁄32in (4mm) clear glass eyes that I bought online very cheaply (see Suppliers on page 141). I decided to mount my fish on a piece of burr (driftwood would also look good); it was attached using a small pin. Finally, after sanding, I polished it with wax polish.

Polar bear cub

DEPENDING ON YOUR PERSPECTIVE, A POLAR BEAR IS EITHER CUTE AND CUDDLY OR, MORE REALISTICALLY, A VERY EFFICIENT HUNTER NOT TO BE UNDERESTIMATED. IT IS THE ONLY ANIMAL ON EARTH FOR WHOM MAN IS A NATURAL PREY: IT WILL SEEK OUT AND ATTACK WITH LITTLE OR NO WARNING. A MARINE ANIMAL, IT IS A VERY GOOD SWIMMER AND CAN BE EQUALLY AT HOME ON LAND OR ICE AND SNOW. IT CAN ALSO MOVE INCREDIBLY QUICKLY.

Having been part of a team that carved a 5,511lb (2.5-tonne) life-sized polar bear for the National Memorial Arboretum in a rather aggressive pose, I decided that I would tackle something a little more endearing this time. This project is inspired by a small, roly-poly netsuke that my wife Em carved some years ago. It is a young polar bear cub rolling in the snow, just for the fun of it. You can make it whatever size you like and from whatever wood you have available.

TOOLBOX

- Lime wood block, 2 x 2 x 3⅛in (50 x 50 x 80mm), or whatever size you wish
- Pencil
- Paper or card
- Safety glove
- Band saw or coping saw
- Knife
- Selection of small palm gouges
- Abrasives
- Drill
- Black buffalo horn
- White acrylic paint or wood bleach (optional)
- Black acrylic paint

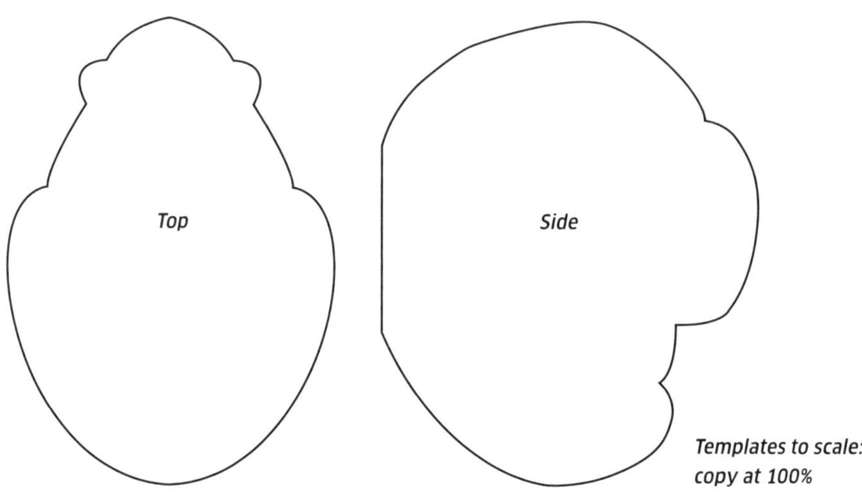

Templates to scale: copy at 100%

1 Draw the patterns onto your block, then cut away any waste. This can be done with a band saw or coping saw, but as there isn't a great deal of waste to be removed, you may prefer to use only your knife. You need to end up with something that is vaguely ball shaped with a flat piece at the bottom.

2 One of the biggest challenges with a carving like this is getting a clear idea of where all the parts of the animal will be located. When it is on its feet, it is not too difficult, but when it is curled up like this, it is a different matter. Spend some time working out where the legs and head are located, especially the various joints. Draw these onto the block as best you can. Don't worry about being too accurate or detailed at this stage.

3 You can now remove some of the obvious waste material using the knife and a small gouge.

4 Once the waste is gone, you should have a better idea of the general shape. Check that everything is in the right place.

5 If you are happy with your progress, you can start with a bit more shaping to make it more 'bear shaped'.

6 Before you continue, you will need some clear reference pictures of polar bears to get an accurate idea of the anatomy, particularly of the legs. These are the closest to the shape of our legs of any common animals. The back legs are not too difficult, but you must be sure where the shoulders are located as well as the elbows. Fortunately, as polar bears have such thick fur, most of the real detail is covered up, so you only need to achieve a general shape.

7 Round off the hind quarters and make sure you have enough wood for the arms.

8 As you can see from these pictures, I tend to draw all over my carvings to make sure I can see where everything goes. You can always erase these marks if necessary, whereas you cannot make too many changes if you have already cut off wood. Keep checking each leg as you carve it to ensure that both the front legs are the same size and the same with the back legs. Slowly and carefully are the bywords here.

9 From now on, it is a matter of rounding everything off and making the whole carving more bear shaped.

10 There is not a great deal of detail to add except to add a bit of texture if you wish, using your knife or some small gouges. My wife carved a polar bear and sanded it very smooth all over. It looked great so you may prefer to do that. For my project, I went over the whole piece with a small shallow gouge to add some fur-like texture.

11 I added some black buffalo horn eyes to this carving (see pages 22–7 for more details on adding eyes). You can polish up the eyes before inserting them but I have found, from experience, that, if I do that, I spend a considerable time scrabblling around on the floor looking for ones I have dropped. In this case, I made up the horn dowel, drilled the holes and inserted it and then cut the horn off, polishing it later in situ.

12 I gave the whole piece a wash of very diluted white acrylic paint just to take away the brownness of the wood. You could also use a wood bleach to achieve this effect. This is very much a personal choice and you may prefer to leave it natural or paint it with a thicker paint for a more realistic look.

13 There are two more small details to finish the piece. Polar bears are actually black – it is only their translucent fur that gives them the white appearance. To acknowledge this, paint the nose and mouth black. You can also use your gouges to add some texturing on the soles of the feet. Although polar bears have black pads, they are seldom very visible as there is a lot of fur under the feet to enable them to get a grip when on ice and snow. Once this is done, your polar bear is complete.

TIP

You should be able to do all the work on this polar bear simply holding the block in your hand but if you prefer to hold it in a clamp or vice, I suggest that you leave a little spare wood at one end to make it easier to hold.

Walrus

THE WALRUS IS IN A FAMILY OF ITS OWN WITH ONLY TWO MEMBERS: THE ATLANTIC WALRUS AND THE PACIFIC WALRUS. BOTH ARE VERY LARGE CREATURES, WITH THE PACIFIC VARIETY WEIGHING UP TO 4,400LB (2 TONNES), LIVING MOSTLY ON CRUSTACEANS AND SMALL MARINE CREATURES. THEY WERE HUNTED WIDELY IN THE 19TH AND 20TH CENTURIES FOR THEIR BLUBBER, SKINS AND TUSKS BUT HAVE MADE A COMEBACK IN MORE RECENT YEARS. THEY ARE VERY HEAVILY BUILT AND ARE MORE AT HOME IN THE ARCTIC AND SUBARCTIC WATERS THAN ON LAND OR MAGAZINE COVERS – THEY ARE NOT REALLY WHAT WE NORMALLY CONSIDER PHOTOGENIC!

I have adapted my design for this project to make what I consider an attractive carving and hope you like the result. If you wish to make a more lifelike version, please feel free to do so. I am sure you can modify the stages I have shown with a little imagination and research.

TOOLBOX

- Lime wood block, 2½ x 2½ x 4in (65 x 65 x 100mm), or whatever size you wish
- Pencil
- Paper or card
- Safety glove
- Band saw or coping saw
- Knife
- Selection of small palm gouges
- Abrasives
- Black wood or buffalo horn
- Pin vice
- Drill
- Finishing oil or wax polish

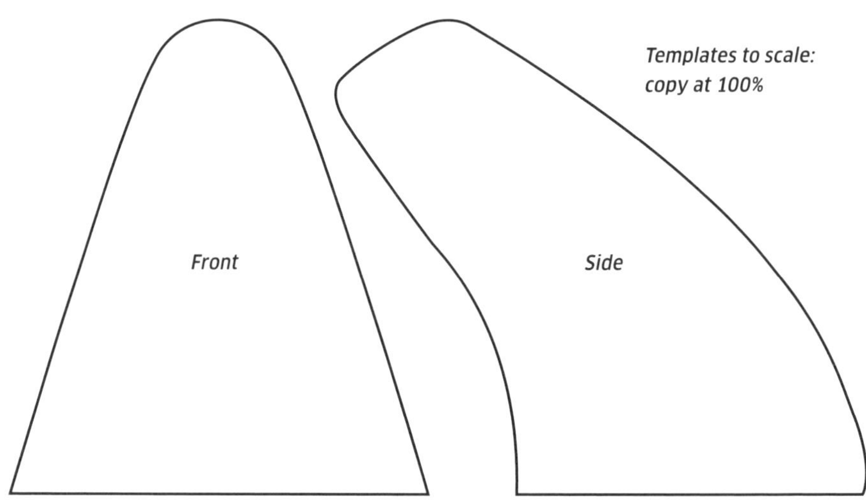

Templates to scale: copy at 100%

1 Draw the two patterns onto your block, marking out the waste to be removed. As there is little real shape in the overall form, you can sketch in a rough shape to cut out and then refine it as you carve. Cut off the waste using a band saw or coping saw. If you use a coping saw, draw the pattern on both sides, carefully matching them up, so that you are cutting squarely across the block. The band saw will automatically cut square. These pictures show the block after the waste has been removed.

2 Next, use your knife to start to refine the overall shape and get rid of the squareness of the block. Then roughly locate and mark the important parts of the body.

3 As there is little real body shape in the walrus, I have tried to give it a bit of a twist to add some interest. I have also slightly reduced the size of the head to give a little more realism.

4 Next, identify and accurately mark where all the parts of the walrus are located. This can involve a lot of measuring and drawing to get everything clear in your head.

5 When you are fairly confident that you have got things in the right places, you can start doing the shaping using your knife.

6 You don't have to carve any muscle detail but you will need to make sure that the head and front flippers are symmetrical.

7 Now it is just a matter of refining what you have already carved using your gouges to add any details.

8 Shape the tusks and add more detail to the flippers. Reference photos will be useful for these details.

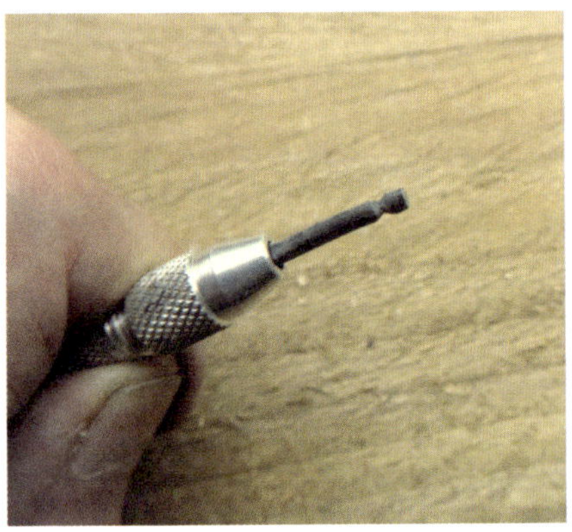

9 Before adding the eyes, give the whole piece a thorough sanding. If you want to add eyes, you can use a piece of black wood or buffalo horn. This will need to be made into a fine dowel about ⅛in (2–3mm) in diameter. This can be done by holding the material in a small pin vice or clamp and scraping or sanding until round (see pages 22–7 for more details about dealing with eyes).

10 Partly cut through about ¼in (5mm) from the end for each eye and drill the head to make the holes for the eyes. Make sure you drill a test hole in a spare piece of wood to ensure that the dowel fits tightly.

11 Test the fit of the dowel before gluing it in place.

12 Once you're satisfied with the fit, put a small drop of adhesive in the socket and push in the dowel until it's firmly in place. Repeat for the other eye.

13 When the glue has set, trim the eye from the dowel and sand until really smooth. You will need to finish with a very fine grit abrasive and then shine up with your finger.

14 Get as smooth a finish as you possibly can and then give the whole piece a coat of finishing oil and wax polish to complete the project.

TIP

I don't advise that you try to texture the body as the walrus is a marine animal and I think it looks much more natural if given a smooth finish. You may think differently, though.

Diving otter

CENTURIES AGO, OTTERS WERE COMMON IN THE UK, BUT THEY WERE WIDELY HUNTED AND THEIR NUMBERS FELL INTO A SERIOUS DECLINE. DUE TO CONSERVATION WORK AND CLEANER WATERWAYS, THEY ARE NOW ENJOYING SOMEWHAT OF A REVIVAL. WITH THEIR VERY PLAYFUL NATURE, THEY ARE A JOY TO WATCH.

For the project, as I haven't got the facility or skill to photograph an otter under water, I have had to study various pictures and videos to put together the information to create a diving pose that I like. If you think that this pose is too complicated, feel free to simplify it.

TOOLBOX

- Basswood block, 1⅝ x 1⅝ x 6in (40 x 40 x 150mm), or whatever size you wish
- Pencil
- Paper or card
- Safety glove
- Knife
- Coping saw or other small saw
- Selection of small palm gouges
- Abrasives
- Block of contrasting wood
- Acrylic water paints (optional)
- Black buffalo horn (optional)
- Pin

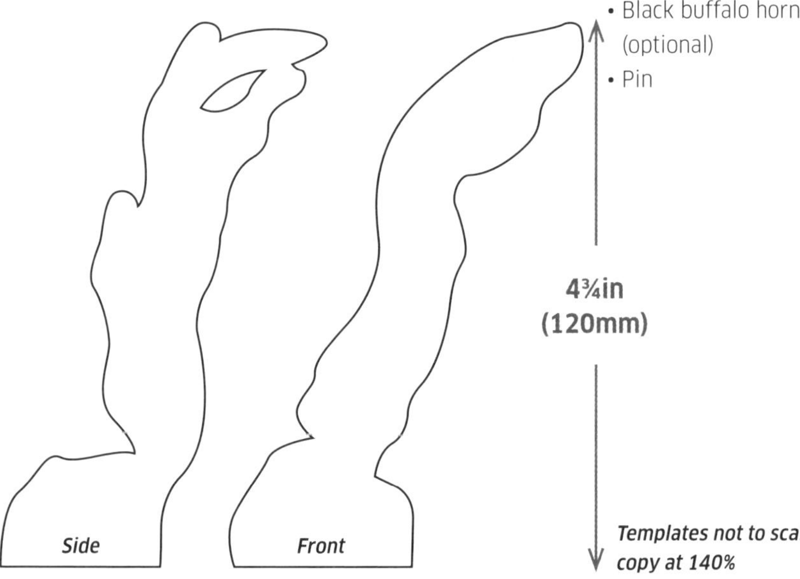

Templates not to scale: copy at 140%

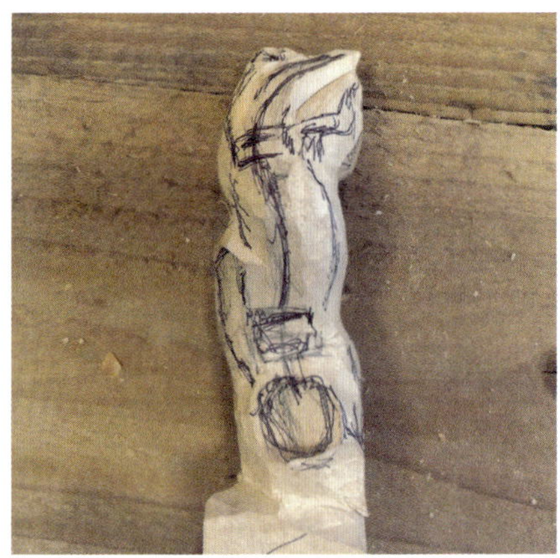

1 For this project, you probably only need to draw one pattern onto your block as too many corners will make it more difficult to produce the necessary twist for this diving pose. I have supplied patterns for the back and side and which you are happier using is up to you.

2 The important objective of the next few stages is to get the twist of the otter's body right and to identify and mark exactly where all parts of the animal will be located. This will involve a lot of drawing and, probably, a lot of rubbing out of the lines you have drawn.

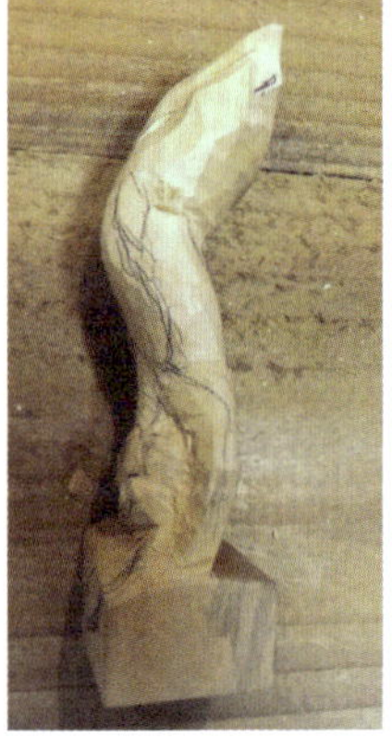

3 Draw the animal as well as you can to show the twist and use your knife to remove any waste wood that you can easily identify.

4 You should end up with a shape that clearly shows the twist of the body but with no real detail.

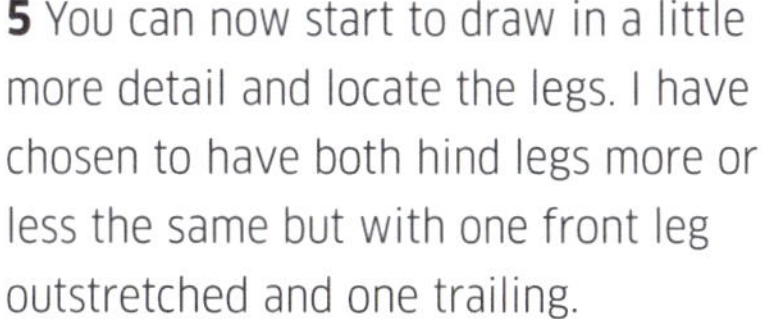

5 You can now start to draw in a little more detail and locate the legs. I have chosen to have both hind legs more or less the same but with one front leg outstretched and one trailing.

6 With your knife, remove as much waste as you can, making sure you can still see the position of each leg but without detail. You might like to also give the head a bit of shape at this point.

7 Now is a good time to add a bit of shape to the legs, checking that each pair of legs are the same size – you are really just making sure that you have enough wood to finish them off later.

8 As this otter is diving, I have added some habitat to support it at the base of the carving, composed of an eel and some rocks. You will need to decide where these will be and mark them on before finally carving the otter as the animal and the base must remain in contact if they are to work successfully.

9 Using your small gouges, work on the legs and slim down the body a little. The otter has a very fat tail so don't slim this down too much. You will almost certainly need some reference pictures of real otters from now on to ensure that all joints are in the correct place.

10 Before turning your attention to the otter's head, I suggest that you give the whole body a good sanding as this will show up any small adjustments that might be necessary.

11 It's a good idea to cut the base as shown so that the whole piece can be mounted on a separate block. You can use a coping saw or any suitable small saw to make this cut.

TIP

When I had almost finished the carving, there was very little wood attaching the otter to the rocks and eel, so I carefully drilled a fine hole up through the rocks and into the otter's head and inserted a long, thin panel pin to give added strength. Even if the carving is not subjected to any sort of rough treatment, the wood is very likely to move or shrink over time, causing a separation. This sort of addition stabilizes the whole piece.

12 Before you go any further with the detailing, I suggest that you fit the carving to a suitable block for a base as you will need to make sure that the carving of the eel and rocks actually fits. Once this is done, you just have to decide what sort of finish you require. I had thought about colouring the whole piece but, after adding some colour to the rocks and eel using acrylic water paints, I decided that I would leave the otter a natural wood colour as it showed the shape more clearly. I also chose to insert some eyes made from small pieces of black buffalo horn (see pages 24–5 for details), but – as always – the choice is yours. Finally, I added another rock to the base to balance the finished carving.

Beaver

THE BEAVER IS A HERBIVOROUS ANIMAL LIVING ON LEAVES, ROOTS, TREE BARK AND WOOD AND, CONTRARY TO GENERAL BELIEF, DOESN'T EAT FISH. ONE OF ITS WELL-KNOWN CHARACTERISTICS IS ITS ABILITY TO RE-ROUTE WATERWAYS BY BUILDING DAMS AND LODGES THAT CAN BE VERY BENEFICIAL TO THE COUNTRYSIDE, HELPING TO PREVENT FLOODING AS WELL AS PROVIDING A HABITAT THAT ENCOURAGES ALL KINDS OF WILDLIFE.

The pose I have chosen is fairly simple and features a beaver carrying a small tree branch. Its feet are simplified as they are seldom seen. You can, of course show it partially submerged to avoid having to do anything about the feet at all.

TOOLBOX

- Basswood block, 1⅝ x 1⅝ x 4¾in (40 x 40 x 120mm), or whatever size you wish
- Pencil
- Paper or card
- Safety glove
- Band saw or coping saw
- Knife
- Selection of small palm gouges
- V-tool
- Wire wool & white vinegar
- Finishing oil or wax polish
- Black paint

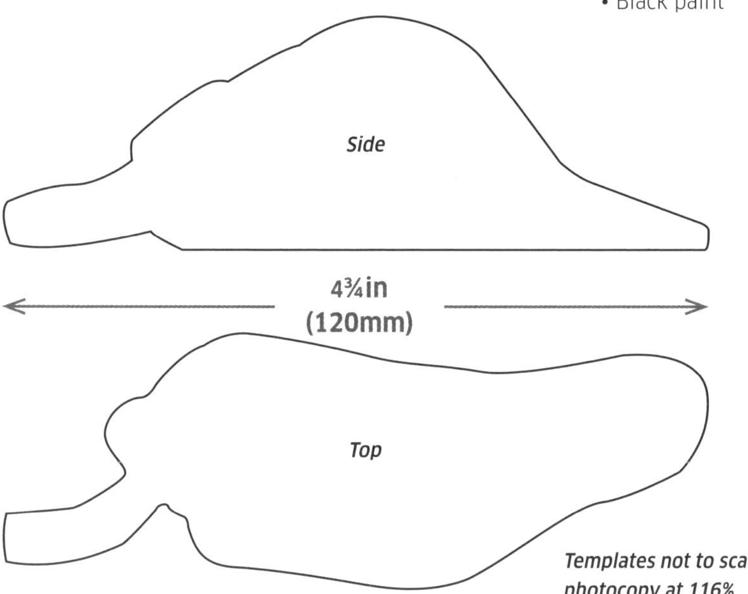

Templates not to scale: photocopy at 116%

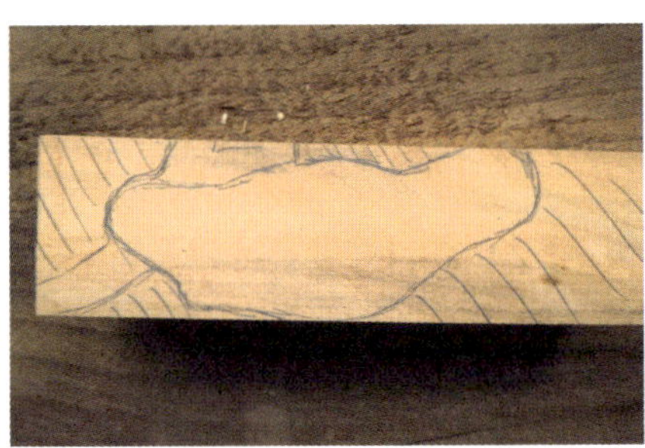

1 Draw the patterns onto your block, making sure that each one is the same distance from the end of the block so that all parts of the animal line up properly.

2 Cut out the shapes you have drawn with a band saw or a coping saw. You can remove this waste with a knife but it will take much longer.

3 This will leave you with a roughly beaver-shaped, squared-off block.

4 Before you remove any more wood, draw as much of the shape of the animal as you can, so that you can get a rough idea of where everything is located. There will be some obvious waste that you can remove first using your knife.

5 You should now have a better idea of the shape.

6 Now you can start to round off all the square edges but ensure that you don't change the overall outline that you drew – you are only removing the 'squareness'.

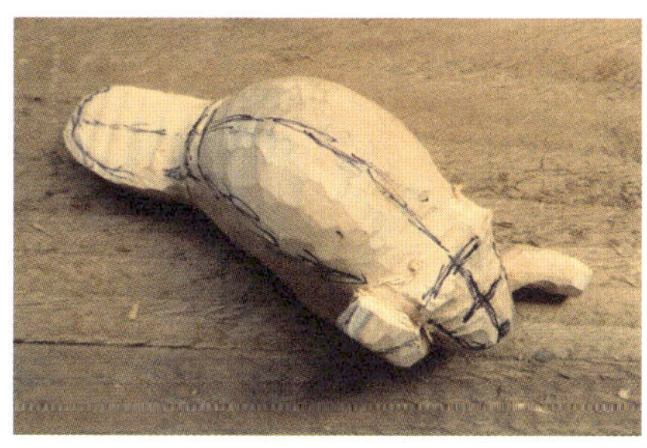

7 It's time to get busy with your pencil to mark out all the finer points that you want to add, especially the shape of the branch that the beaver has in its mouth.

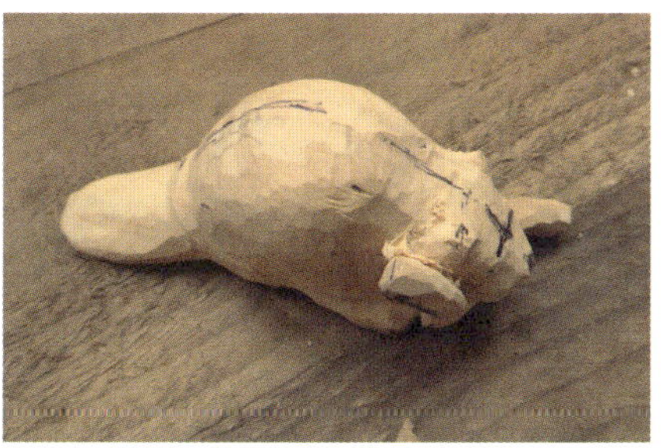

8 Once you have carved out the branch, you will need to take extra care when handling the piece so that you don't accidentally break it off.

9 The basic shape is now established so you can begin to add the finer detail and texture using small gouges or a V-tool. I have not gone to the extent of adding detail to the feet as these are rarely seen above the water, so just general shaping is fine for them.

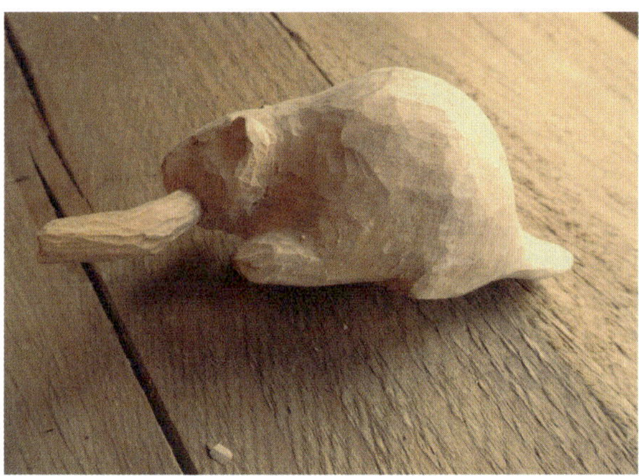

10 The overall impression of this animal is one of a large lump of fur and big teeth, so don't get too carried away with detail!

TIP

When making the solution for the colouring, you can use cola as an alternative to vinegar as you don't get the fish and chip shop smell with that, but the results are the same.

11 Use the gouges or V-tool to add a bit of texture to the branch to create some contrast between that and the beaver's fur.

12 I thought I would add a bit of colour to this carving but didn't want to paint it, so I decided to use a technique that I have used successfully before. Make a solution by adding some wire wool to white vinegar and leaving it to soak for a few days. If you paint the carving with this solution, the wood will turn brown or grey as a result of the chemical reaction between the solution and the tannin in the wood. If you want it darker, you can apply a wet tea bag, which will darken the wood even further, even up to black – see the beaver's tail. I am not sure that I am completely satisfied with the result in this case, but prefer this method to using paint. It is worth a try.

13 Add a coat of finishing oil, paint the eyes with a small spot of black paint and wax the whole piece. You could take things further by adding texture and a bit more detail but that depends on how much time you wish to spend.

Octopus

I HAVE INCLUDED AN OCTOPUS AS IT IS A FASCINATING CREATURE AND QUITE A CHALLENGE TO CARVE. THIS AMAZING ANIMAL IS EXTREMELY INTELLIGENT AND BECAUSE IT HAS NO SKELETON SEEMS ABLE TO ADOPT ALMOST ANY SHAPE. ABLE TO MOVE OVER LAND AS WELL AS IN THE SEA, THERE ARE AROUND 300 DIFFERENT SPECIES, FROM THE TINY WOLFI OCTOPUS WEIGHING LESS THAN 1G (0.04OZ) AND MEASURING 1IN (2.5CM) IN LENGTH TO THE GIANT PACIFIC OCTOPUS, WHERE ONE RECORD-SMASHING SPECIMEN SUPPOSEDLY WEIGHED A WHOPPING 600LB (272KG) AND MEASURED 30FT (9M) LONG.

An octopus has eight long tentacles with hundreds of suckers underneath that you can carve if you wish (although you will need specialist power tools to get a good result), a large roundish body, two eyes and a web shape between the body and tentacles. You can arrange the carving as you like but it will need to be supported by rocks or something similar as it will be very fragile when completed. While carving this, I realized that it is not really a project for the faint-hearted, so have kept the shape fairly simple and stylized, but you can be as adventurous as you like.

TOOLBOX

- Lime or basswood block, 2 x 2 x 6in (50 x 50 x 150mm)
- Pencil
- Paper or card
- Safety glove
- Band saw or coping saw
- Knife
- Abrasives
- Selection of palm gouges; No.4, 3mm fishtail gouge is recommended
- Scalpel
- Procion fabric dye (optional)
- Black paint
- Finishing oil or wax polish

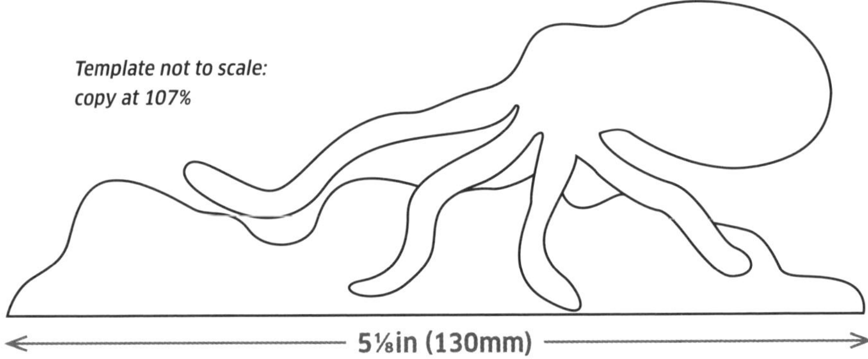

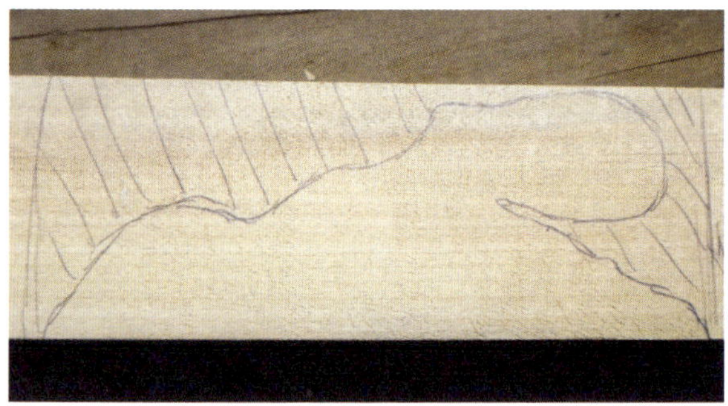

1 Draw the pattern onto your block and shade in the waste to be removed.

2 Cut out the outline with a band saw or coping saw, removing the waste you have shaded in.

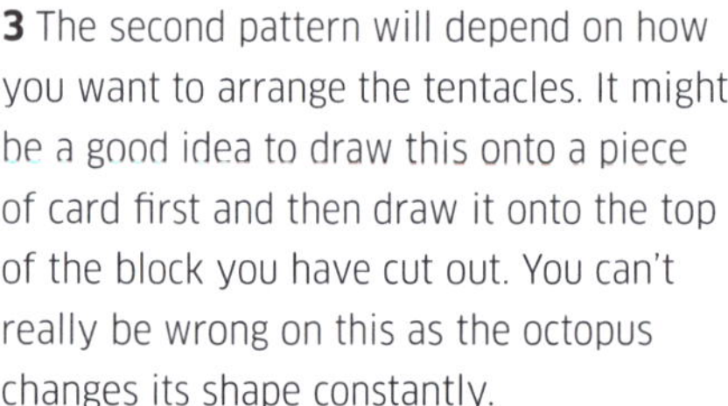

3 The second pattern will depend on how you want to arrange the tentacles. It might be a good idea to draw this onto a piece of card first and then draw it onto the top of the block you have cut out. You can't really be wrong on this as the octopus changes its shape constantly.

4 Cut out the body of the octopus using your knife, leaving the wood underneath for the rear tentacles.

5 Decide where you want the tentacles to be. Note that there should be eight of them in total, all of the same length, and that you are going to have to carve them, so don't make them too complicated. They do get very thin at the ends so you need to arrange them so that they support each other, especially at the back where there are no rocks. I have left the design that way as, if there were rocks under the body, it would be almost impossible to carve the tentacles as the body would be in the way.

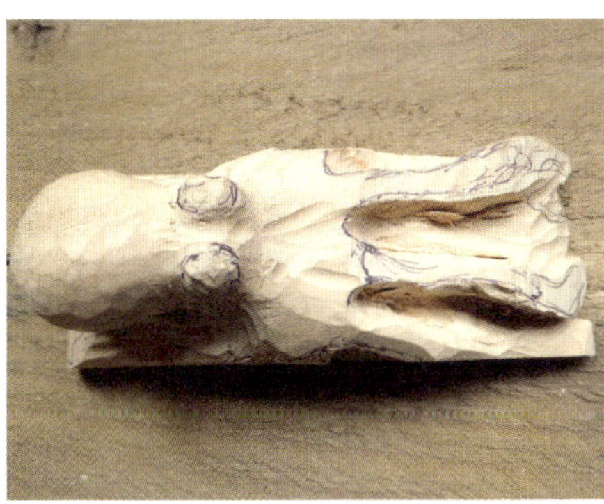

6 Once you have a rough idea where you want the tentacles, you can start to rough them out using the knife. Concentrate on the direction that each one will follow but don't cut them to length at this stage as you will need to match them up as you go.

7 Carefully arrange the rear tentacles. You will need to bend these around a bit to be make them the same length as the front ones. Drawing a line down the middle of each one will help to get a smooth curve where needed.

8 Sanding the tentacles as you work will help to keep the lines softer and make it easier to check for length.

9 Much of the work on the rear end will need to be done from the underside but be careful not to separate the tentacles. Don't narrow down any of them at this stage as there is still quite a bit to do and you don't want to break any of the ends off.

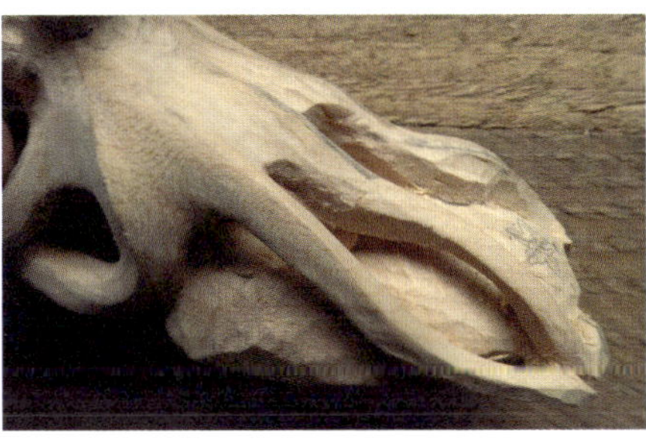

10 Go over each of the eight tentacles and check for length. You might need to curl the ends on some to increase their length or even hide the end under a rock. It is not so much a matter of fine measurement, it is more about them all looking about the same. Even just slimming them down on the inside or outside of a curve can make a difference in the length.

11 Clean up the rocks and continue with the sanding, drawing in any additional detail that you want to include in the project.

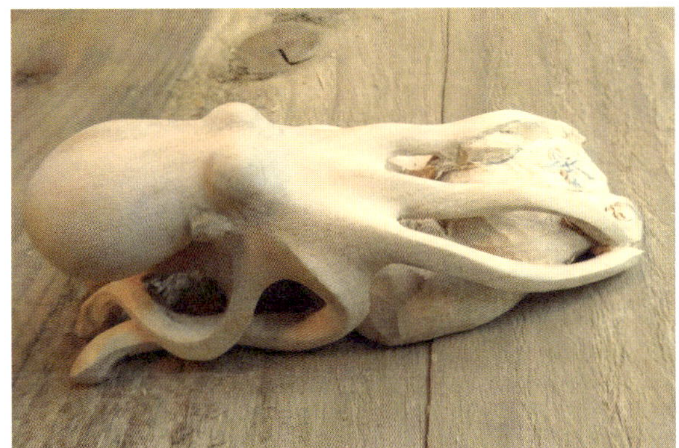

12 I decided to add a small crab and a starfish, but you can add what you like or even nothing at all.

13 Using the gouges, you can carve this extra detail ready to start the final sanding before adding the eyes. A scalpel is especially useful for the finer details. Although an octopus is by no means smooth, I have decided that this one is to be slightly stylized with a very smooth, shiny finish, and with no suckers on the tentacles. You can make your own choices.

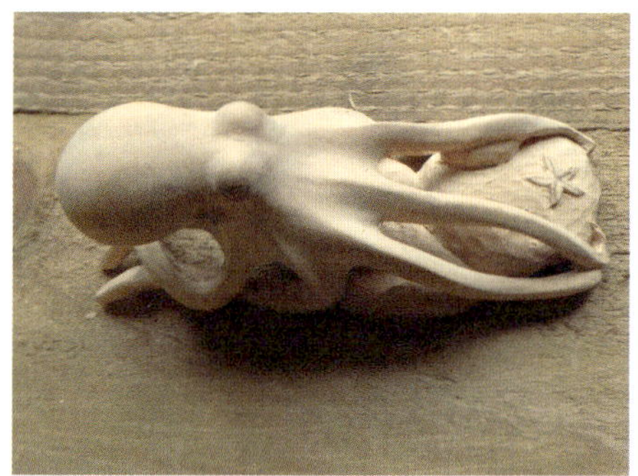

14 This next stage needs to be carried out very carefully. Slim down each tentacle as much as you feel you can do safely. Then sand it smooth along its length, leaving the rock with a tooled finish. Each tentacle has a raised ridge along its length down the centre of the top. If you are not carving the suckers, leave the underside smooth and flat. If you break one of the tentacles, you can always glue it back on and re-sand it but you will probably need to paint it afterwards to hide the join. It can still look great when painted (maybe even better!) but I decided to colour just the rocks as a contrast. To do this, I used a very small quantity of Procion fabric dye. This is easy to use, without a tendency to bleed into the surrounding wood.

15 You can now carve the eyes. Octopus eyes vary considerably so I chose a basic shape. See pages 22-7 for more details on this method.

16 All that is now left to do is to paint the eyes and, after a final fine sanding, give the whole carving a few coats of finishing oil. You can then leave it as it is or mount it on a wooden plinth to give extra protection to the tentacles.

TIP

If you want to be really adventurous, you could use a piece of burr wood for this carving. It would make a stunning piece with the grain patterns that you can find in burrs.

Diving sea lion

THIS PROJECT IS A LITTLE DIFFERENT FROM THE PREVIOUS ONES. THE DESIGN IS REALLY INTENDED AS A STARTING-OFF POINT FOR YOU TO ADAPT AS YOU WISH, RATHER THAN FOLLOW EXACTLY. IT IS NOT FOR THE FAINT-HEARTED AND WILL NEED CONSIDERABLE SIMPLIFICATION IF YOU'RE A BEGINNER.

As with the kingfisher (see pages 132–9), the idea is to carve a diving creature; what else you add is entirely up to you. I made my additions quite complicated to give you more inspiration, but as long as the sea lion and water are supported, you can do as much as you wish.

As seals and sea lions can often be found in close proximity to vegetation, I have decided to include this in my design to add a bit of realism. You can change the position of the plants as long as they provide the necessary support for the animal.

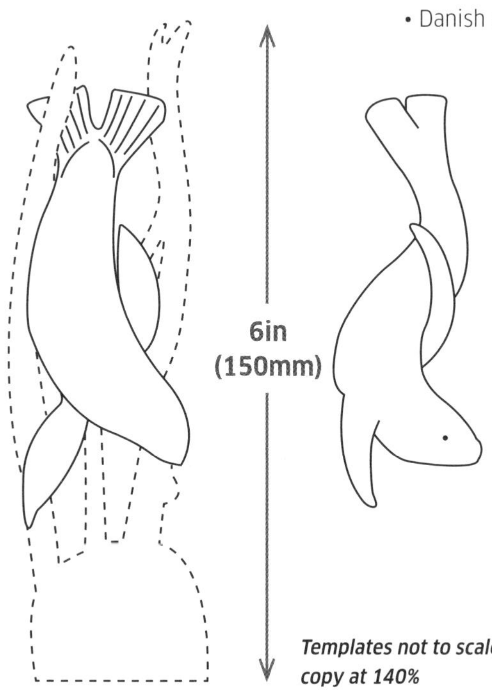

Templates not to scale: copy at 140%

TOOLBOX

- Basswood or lime wood block, 1⅝ x1⅝ x 6in (40 x 40 x 150mm), or whatever size you wish
- Pencil
- Paper or card
- Safety glove
- Coping saw or other small saw
- Knife
- Selection of palm gouges
- Abrasives
- Drill and small pins (optional)
- Danish oil and wax polish

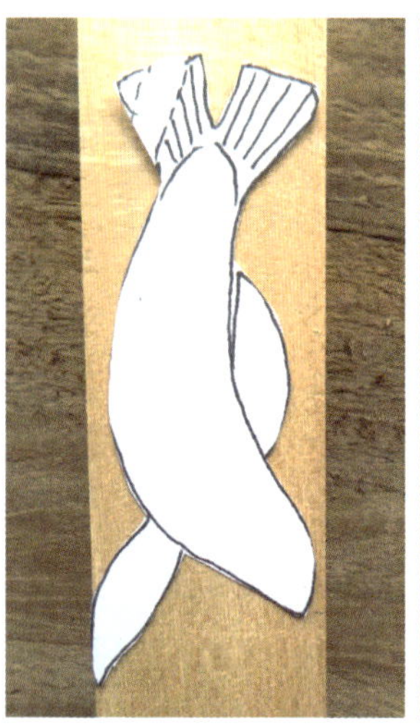

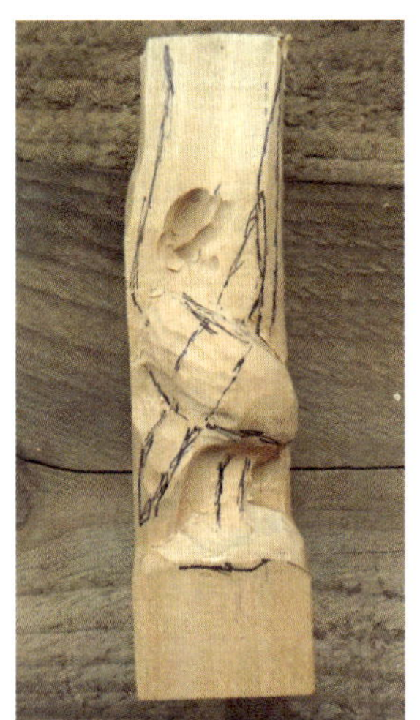

1 The pattern shows the basic shape of the sea lion as this is the focal point of the carving – whatever else you include (vegetation, other creatures, etc) is up to you. Start by drawing the patterns onto your block to give you an idea where the animal will be. Obviously, as you carve you will remove the lines you have drawn, so to start with you will be drawing and redrawing many times before you get the shape anywhere near right.

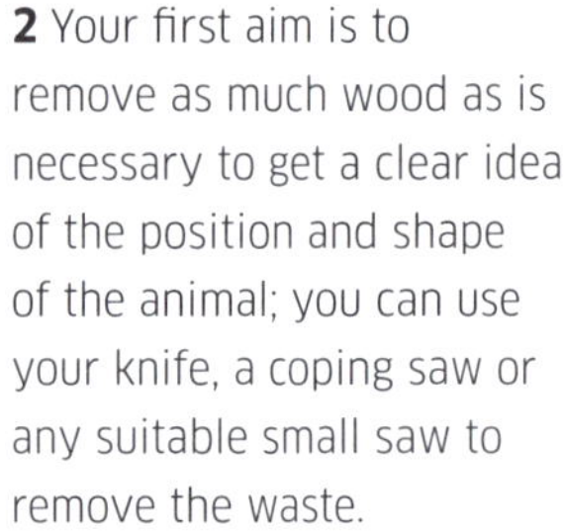

2 Your first aim is to remove as much wood as is necessary to get a clear idea of the position and shape of the animal; you can use your knife, a coping saw or any suitable small saw to remove the waste.

3 As you do this, bear in mind that you will have to leave space for the weeds that support the sea lion. Don't concentrate only on the sea lion; the weeds are equally important.

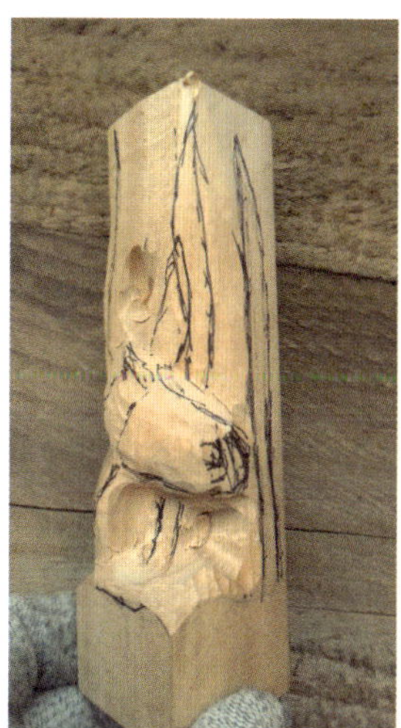

4 The parts of the sea lion that are easily overlooked are the fins. Keep drawing: it doesn't really matter where the fins are as long as they are attached in the right place.

TIP

The problem with carving something that lives all or part of its life in the water is how you support it so that it looks as though it is swimming. I have seen carved sharks, whales and dolphins mounted on brass or wooden rods attached to a base in what is supposed to be a swimming position and, somehow, they never look right. To be honest, I have produced some of these myself, but never with any real satisfaction.

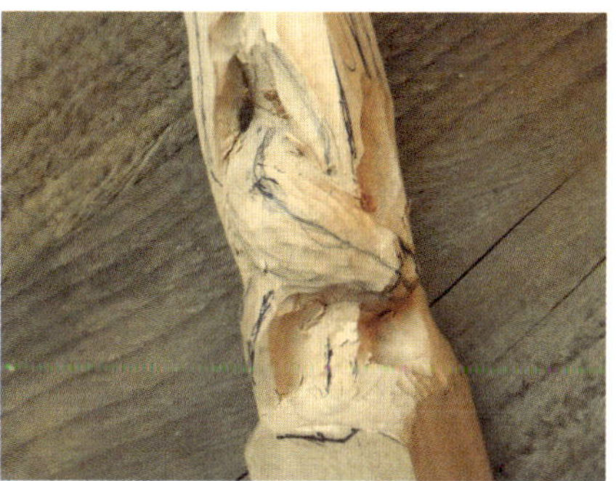

5 One of the problems you will encounter is making sure that the view from the front ties in with the views from the other sides. You will find that making holes where there will obviously be space will help in tying it all together. At the same time, be careful not to make any holes in the body of the sea lion.

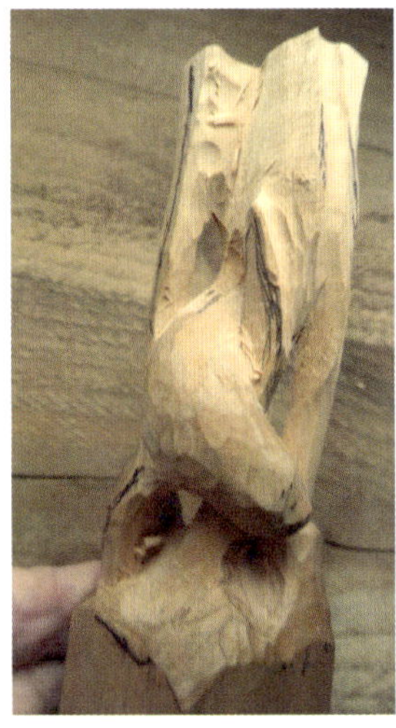

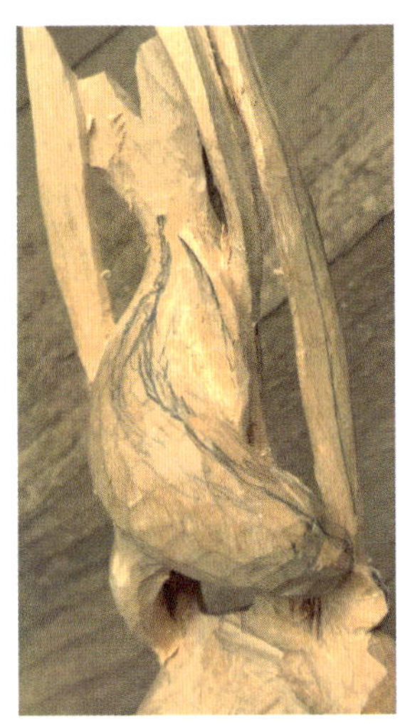

6 At this point, it's worth concentrating on shaping the sea lion's body as much as you can. As you do this, you will need to also constantly check on the shape of the weeds; you will need to keep at least some of the weeds in contact with the sea lion in order to give the animal the necessary support.

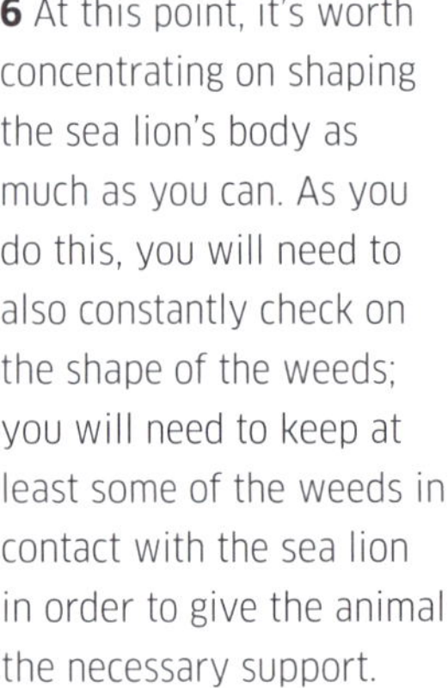

9 Don't forget that there is one flipper behind the animal's body and you will need to leave enough wood for that.

8 You can now draw in any additional detail on and around the body that you might like to include.

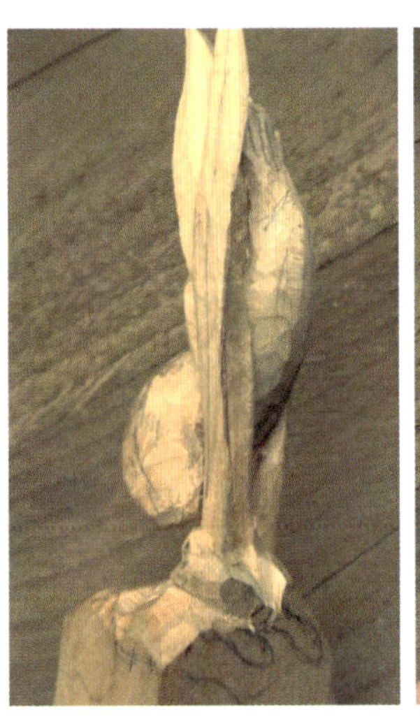

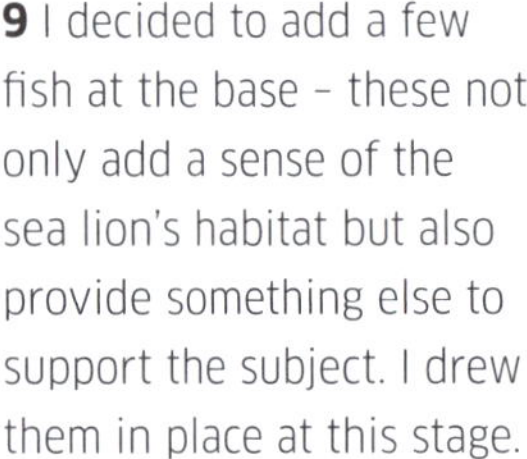

9 I decided to add a few fish at the base – these not only add a sense of the sea lion's habitat but also provide something else to support the subject. I drew them in place at this stage.

10 I suggest that you refer to some pictures of sea lions now as you will need to spend some time refining the shape and removing waste wood. While you do this, keep in mind that the weeds and other detail have to support the animal. This can be a slow and careful process as there is a risk of crushing any fine detail that you have carved as you go along.

11 Before adding the finishing touches to the sea lion, concentrate on completing all the added detail that is to be included. In my case this is a selection of rocks and pebbles with the three fish and the weeds already shown. Pay extra attention to the parts that are in contact with the animal as they are necessary for support. Use a selection of small gouges to add the details and textures.

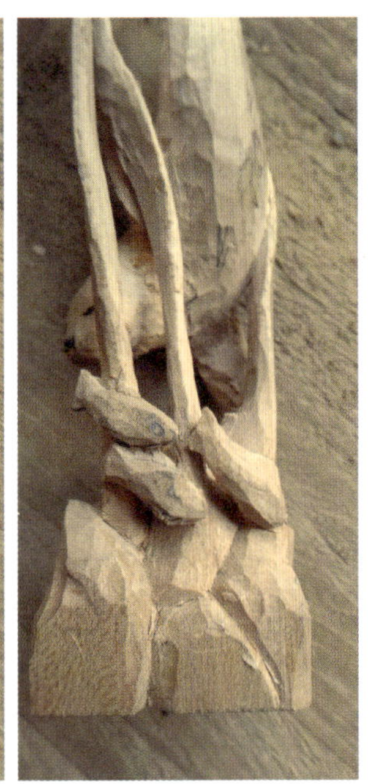

12 Now comes the most delicate and tedious part of the whole process: giving the animal, fish and weeds a thorough sanding. You will need to go through the grades of abrasive to remove any tool marks or scratches, finishing with something like 600 grit. You might need to use a small lolly stick or toothpick, with abrasive wrapped round it, to get into the difficult areas. I left the rocks with a tooled finish as a contrast.

13 Once I felt that I had got everything smooth, I gave the whole piece a coat of Danish oil as this shows up any areas that might need further attention. When I was happy with the results, I added the eyes. In this case, I decided to use some small pins for the sea lion and simply made small holes for the fishes' eyes. You can, of course, use whatever method you choose (see pages 22–7 for more ideas). Give the whole thing a coat of wax polish and you are done.

Diving kingfisher

AROUND THE WORLD THERE ARE MANY BIRDS THAT CAN BE SEEN MAKING SPECTACULAR DIVES INTO WATER TO CATCH FISH. IN THE UK THESE SIGHTINGS TEND TO BE LIMITED TO AREAS AROUND THE COASTLINE, BUT YOU MAY GET A CHANCE TO SPOT A KINGFISHER NEAR YOUR LOCAL RIVER OR STREAM. YOU WILL HAVE TO BE EXTREMELY LUCKY, AS THE BIRD IS VERY SMALL AND FAST AND OFTEN ALL YOU WILL SEE IS A FLEETING FLASH OF BRIGHT BLUE OUT OF THE CORNER OF YOUR EYE.

In order to end up with a carving that is not too small, I have decided to place the bird at an angle on a block of lime. My project is intended as a starting-off point for your own ideas, so you may prefer to change the size and angle. The pattern I've provided is only for the bird; anything else is down to you and what you think you can achieve. As the bird is so small, I have taken a few liberties with the scale of parts of the piece to make a better all-round effect.

TOOLBOX

- Lime block, 2 x 2 x 5½in (50 x 50 x 140mm), or whatever size you wish
- Pencil
- Paper or card
- Safety glove
- Band saw or coping saw
- Knife
- Try square
- Selection of small palm gouges; 2 x No.9 in different sizes, No.3 or No.4 are recommended
- Scalpel
- V-tool
- Abrasives
- Finishing oil

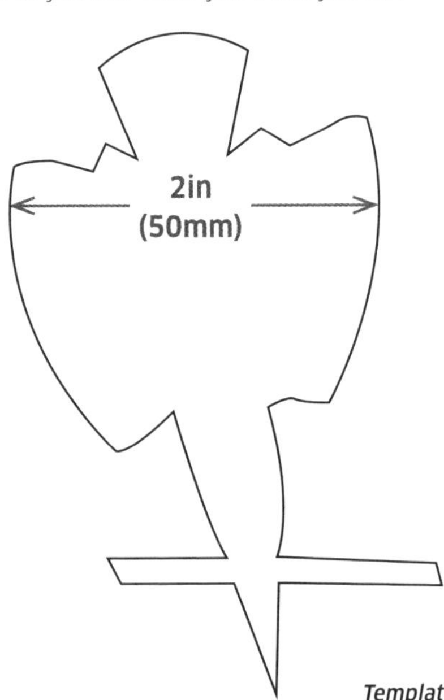

Template not to scale: copy at 110%

1 Start by cutting the wood for the bird at an angle as shown here using a band saw or coping saw.

TIP

As the kingfisher is going to end up being supported only by its head in the water, it's best to leave the water as thick as you can while carving. You can thin it down at the end. Reeds and plants are added for strength and to support the water and fish. These will be carved as I progress, depending on what wood is available. I would add that this is a far from easy project. I have shown what I have included as a guide but you can make this as simple or complicated as you wish.

2 Mark the outline of the bird in pencil, as clearly as you can, from the pattern, bearing in mind that you may well wish to reduce the size as you go along.

3 Cut the outline you have drawn using a coping saw or similar small hand saw. A band saw would not be suitable for this as the bird is set at an angle.

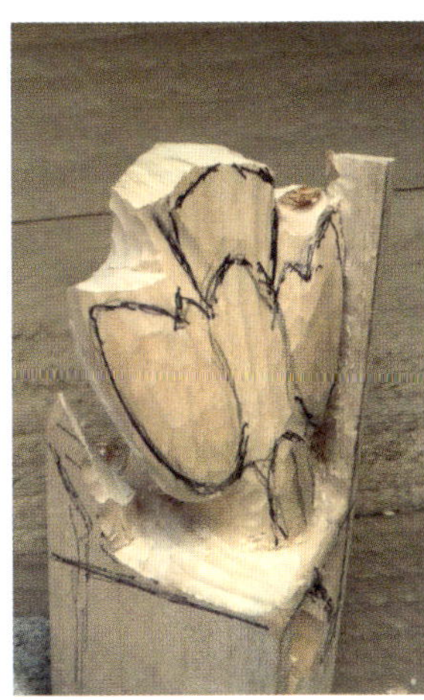

4 You can now start to clear some of the waste wood from around the bird using the knife. Only remove enough to be able to reach all parts of the bird with your tools. Any wood left can be used for any extra elements s you might want to add to your composition and to support the water.

5 It was at this stage that I felt that the bird was too big for the surroundings so I reduced the overall size – only by a little, but I was not sure if I would need to reduce it even more.

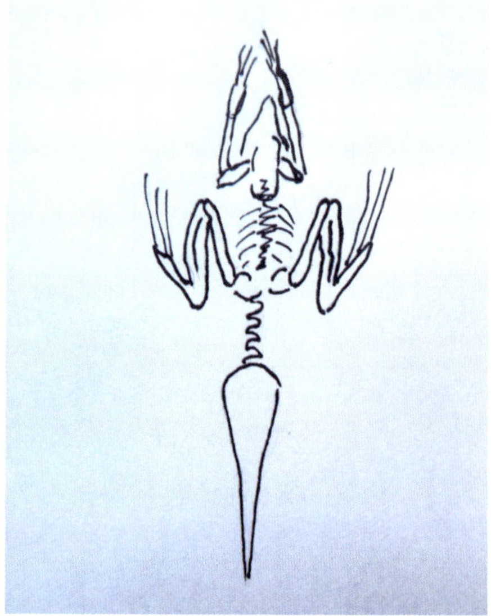

6 I redrew the bird at this stage, marking in the bones of the wings – check with the skeleton drawing to see where they are placed.

7 Using a try square or similar, draw in the water level all around and start to thin this down a little on three sides, leaving the area alone at the back, as this will be ground. I decided to use the larger area of waste wood on the corner as a small broken sign but you can make it what you wish (or remove it altogether).

8 Now draw in the rest of the detail you wish to add so that you know where everything will be in the finished carving. This also gives you the chance to remove all the rest of the waste wood ready for slimming everything down and adding the fine detail.

9 How much more you add to the carving is very much a matter of choice. I have included quite a lot of detail to give you some ideas but be aware that some of it is not easy to do. Use your small palm gouges to carve these details; the scalpel is the best tool for the very fine details.

10 Once you have decided what to include, you can concentrate on finishing the bird. It is too small to add much feather detail, so I suggest that you give a general idea by adding a bit of detail and texture. Use the V-tool to suggest the feather texture.

11 Now everything can be refined. I suggest that you sand the weed, fish and pebbles, leaving the rest with a clean, tooled finish. Check it all over and try to remove as many 'fuzzies' and rough areas as you can (without risking breaking any detail off), and give it all a couple of coats of finishing oil. This will give it a protective finish as well as some strengthening of the more vulnerable parts. I chose not to wax polish it as I got it so far without any breakage and didn't wish to push my luck!

12 If your carving is not the same as mine when you are finished, don't worry; the more of yourself you put into this (or any of the projects), the better. As long as you are happy, everything else is fine.

TIP

If you are wondering what to do about the bird's eyes, rest easy – kingfishers close their eyes when fishing so all you need to do is create a small shadow to show where the eyes are. This can be done when everything else is finished.

Summary

WITH THESE PROJECTS I HAVE TRIED TO INCLUDE AS MANY CARVING SKILLS, TECHNIQUES AND CHALLENGES AS I CAN. SOME OF THESE YOU MAY WELL KNOW ALREADY WHILE OTHERS MAY BE BEYOND YOUR SKILLS RIGHT NOW BUT MAY WELL PROVE VALUABLE FOR FUTURE PROJECTS.

I have also had the opportunity to try a variety of different knives that I hadn't had experience of using before. Although I have come to the conclusion that any of the projects could have been completed with any of the knives, I have obviously developed my own preferences. If the projects had been attempted one at a time, with plenty of rest in between, the small penknife would have been quite adequate. If you did them all one after another, however, you would definitely need to use a variety of knives to prevent pain in your hands.

If I was carving away from home and needed a folding knife, I would choose a small penknife and the Ross Oar whittling knife – one very cheap and one quite expensive. While it is very useful, I found the multi-knife with the side gouges difficult to get used to but, if it suits you, and you can get it at the right price, it is a very useful tool when on the move.

For carving in your own home without the need to follow legal requirements, you may well find, as I did, that homemade knives with handles shaped to suit your hand are the best option. You can choose the blade shapes you want as well. For prolonged carving sessions you will have the option of changing knives regularly to avoid hand cramps.

I would certainly avoid buying more than one knife with a particular handle pattern and suggest you start with a very simple, plain handle shape – you can always modify it if required.

My overall conclusion is to start simple with your tools and carving and see how changes can be made to improve matters. The ideal tool has nothing to do with design, shape or cost; it is about what feels good and does what you need it to do. Most of all it needs to be kept sharp. Happy carving!

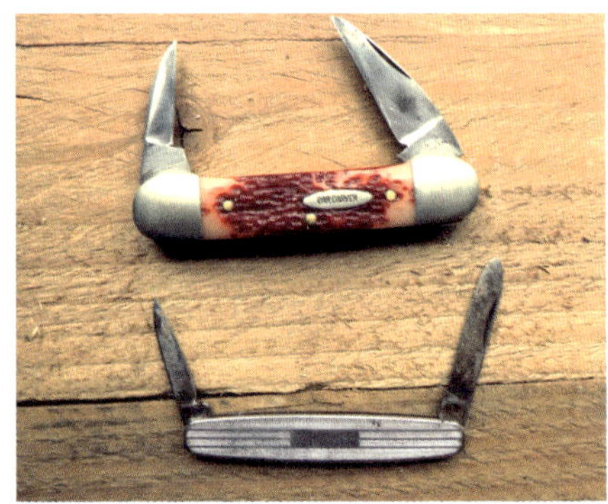

Suppliers

THE THINKING BEHIND THIS BOOK IS THAT YOU CAN TACKLE ALL THE PROJECTS USING THE MINIMUM OF TOOLS AND EQUIPMENT. THIS MEANS THAT YOU DON'T NEED TO SPEND A GREAT DEAL OF MONEY IN ORDER TO GET STARTED. AS MENTIONED ELSEWHERE, YOU COULD WELL GET A SUITABLE KNIFE FROM A THRIFT OR CHARITY SHOP FOR NEXT TO NOTHING – THE IMPORTANT THING IS THAT IT IS COMFORTABLE TO USE AND EASY TO KEEP SHARP. COST HAS LITTLE TO DO WITH IT.

The suppliers listed here are ones that I have used personally, or have known for years, and have always supplied goods of a high standard.

IN THE UK

Knives

Cyclaire knives
cyclaireshop.co.uk

Moonraker Knives
moonrakerknives.co.uk

Nic Westermann
nicwestermann.co.uk

Rutlands
rutlands.com

General tools

Classic Hand Tools
classichandtools.com

Henry Taylor
henrytaylortools.co.uk

Workshop Heaven
workshopheaven.com

Micro tools

Ashley Iles: micro gouges as well as a full range of carving tools
ashleyilestoolstore.co.uk

Metal Clay: Dockyard Tools micro carving tools
metalclay.co.uk

Basswood blocks

Andrew Legge
Email: andrewlegge7@gmail.com

Glass eyes

Snowdonia Supplies
snowdoniasupplies.co.uk

The Makerss
themakerss.co.uk

Also **etsy.com** and **amazon.co.uk**

IN THE USA

Knives and carving tools

Belcher Carving Supply
belchercarvingsupply.com

Greg Dorrance
gregdorrance.com

Kryshak knives
kryshakcarvingtools.com

Mastercarver
mastercarver.com

R. Murphy Knives
rmurphyknives.com

Stadtlander Woodcarving
stadtlandercarvings.com

Note: There are regulations covering the purchase of knives both from a shop and online. Please check before purchasing.

About the author

PETER BENSON SPENT HIS WORKING LIFE TEACHING PHYSICAL EDUCATION AND OTHER GENERAL SUBJECTS, FINISHING BY RUNNING A SPECIAL EDUCATIONAL NEEDS DEPARTMENT. THIS PERIOD OF HIS LIFE CONVINCED HIM THAT ANYONE CAN DO ALMOST ANYTHING WITH THE RIGHT MOTIVATION AND OPPORTUNITY.

On his retirement in 1996, Peter set up the Essex School of Woodcarving, and then spent the next 20 years teaching people to carve all around the country. During this period he also made many trips to the United States, France, Canada and Australia, visiting clubs and organizing workshops. Peter spent 14 years as Chairman of the British Woodcarvers Association and headed a group of enthusiastic carvers producing large carved memorials, including a 5,511lb (2.5-tonne) life-sized polar bear, for the National Memorial Arboretum in Staffordshire, UK.

Peter's passion has always been carving in miniature, especially the Japanese art of netsuke, and he is the author of *The Art of Carving Netsuke* (GMC Publications, 2010). He is also the author of *Whittling Handbook*, *Woodland Whittling*, *Whittling Woodland Animals* and *Whittling Walking Sticks*, all published by GMC Publications.

Peter is a regular contributor to and frequent Guest Editor of *Woodcarving* magazine and is always in demand for advice on woodcarving. He also volunteers at his local primary school teaching small groups of children how to carve.

Index

First published 2025 by
Guild of Master Craftsman Publications Ltd
Castle Place, 166 High Street, Lewes,
East Sussex, BN7 1XU, UK

ISBN 978 1 78494 694 4

A catalogue record for this book is available from the British Library.

Publisher: Jonathan Bailey
Production: Jim Bulley
Senior Project Editor: Sara Harper
Editor: Jane Roe
Design Manager: Robin Shields
Photography: Andrew Perris, Peter Benson and Em Benson

Colour origination by GMC Reprographics
Printed and bound in China

To order a book, contact: **GMC Publications Ltd**
Castle Place, 166 High Street, Lewes, East Sussex
BN7 1XU, United Kingdom
Tel: +44 (0)1273 488005
www.gmcbooks.com

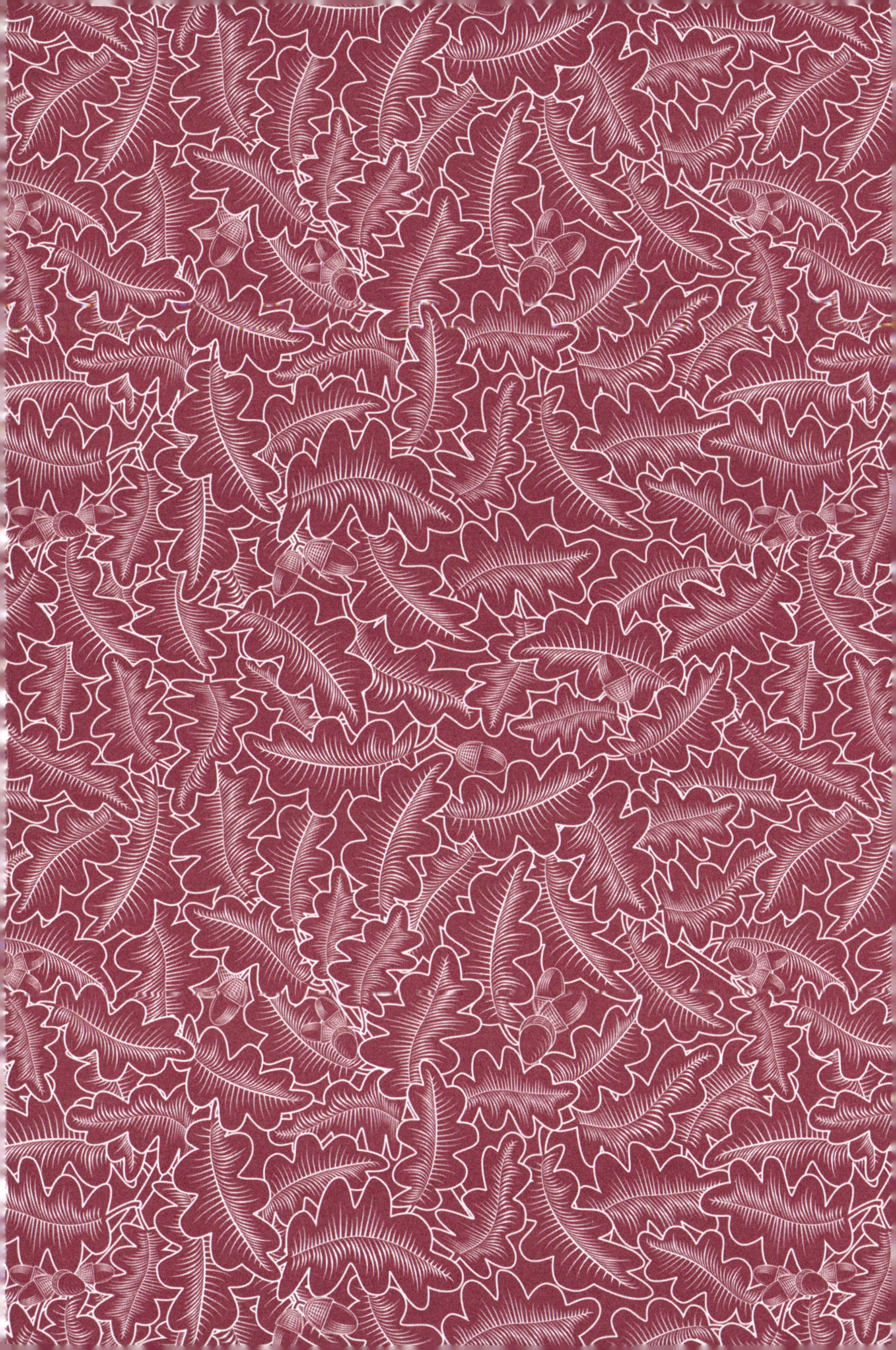

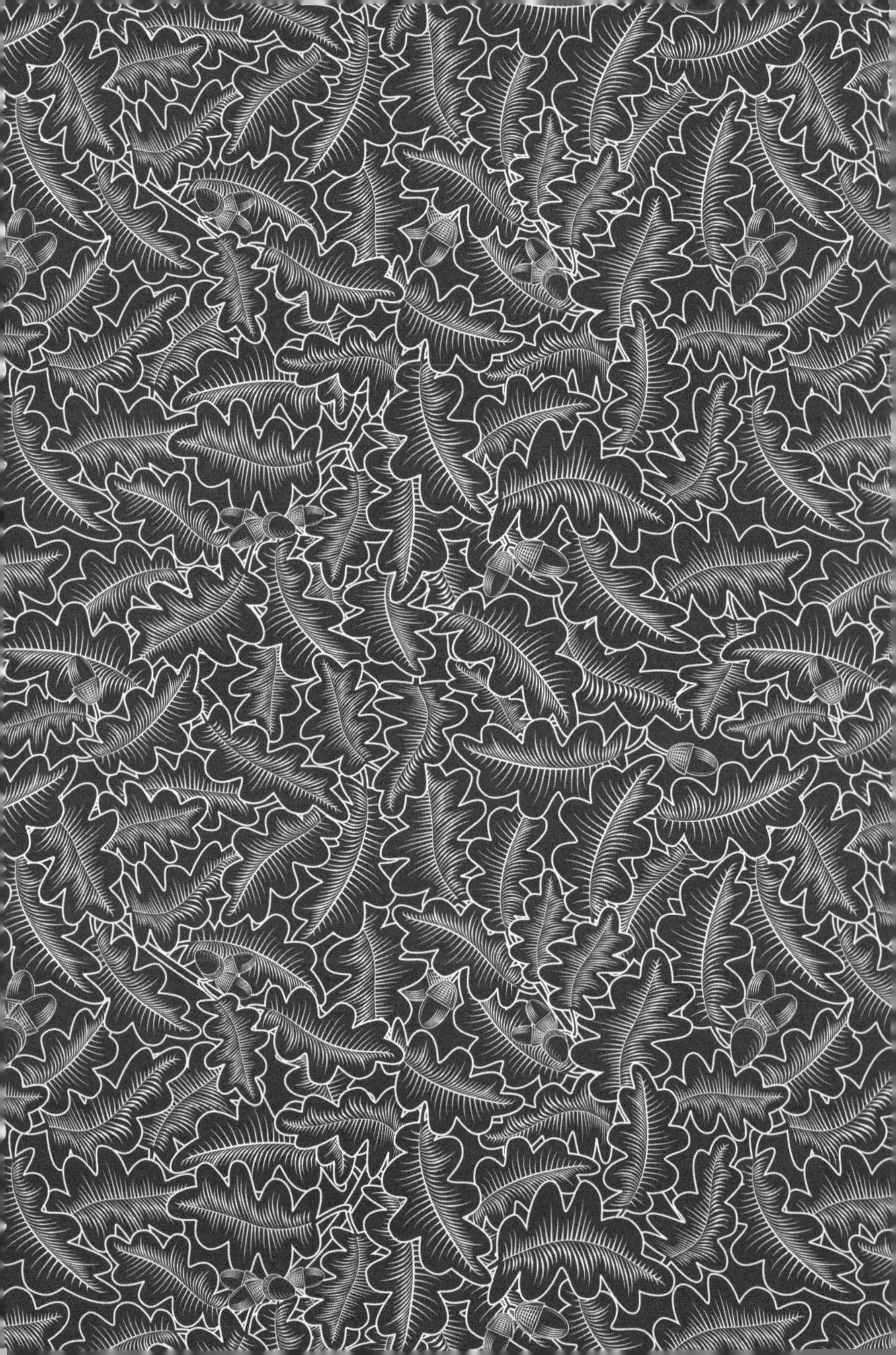